Maximizing Children's Memory Potential

In *Maximizing Children's Memory Potential*, cognitive psychologist Emily M. Elliott bridges the crucial gap between research and real-world application, providing an accessible and entertaining overview of how memory and attention function together in children. This book demystifies the complex workings of these interconnected cognitive systems while offering practical, scientifically based strategies to enhance learning outcomes.

The book tackles essential topics, including the distinctions between short-term, working, and long-term memory, the role of attention in learning, and the surprising benefits of forgetting. Most importantly, it reviews myths about memory and attention, such as the persistent and harmful myth of learning styles, and describes how these myths can be detrimental to successful learning. The content is enriched with real-world applications, addressing modern challenges including the rapidly evolving role of technology and artificial intelligence on cognitive functioning, emphasizing that learning to think about thinking and to evaluate information will be an increasingly important skill as AI tools continue to evolve.

This essential resource is designed for professionals who work directly with school-aged children, including teachers, school administrators, mental health counselors, school counselors, and social workers. It is equally valuable for families and other adults seeking to support children's academic success and learning potential in an increasingly complex learning environment.

Emily M. Elliott is a Professor of Cognitive Psychology at Louisiana State University in the US. She studies the development of memory and attention in children, with a special interest in how sounds affect cognition.

Maximizing Children's Memory Potential

Science-Based Strategies for Learning Success

Emily M. Elliott

Routledge
Taylor & Francis Group
NEW YORK AND LONDON

Designed cover image: Getty images

First published 2027
by Routledge
605 Third Avenue, New York, NY 10158

and by Routledge
4 Park Square, Milton Park, Abingdon, Oxon, OX14 4RN

Routledge is an imprint of the Taylor & Francis Group, an informa business

ISBN: 9781041140641 (hbk)
ISBN: 9781041140610 (pbk)
ISBN: 9781003672814 (ebk)

DOI: 10.4324/9781003672814

Typeset in Optima
by Newgen Publishing UK

This book is dedicated to my family, and especially my grandmothers, Vernice Richard and Sue Elliott. They were phenomenal role models and helped to shape me into the person I am today.

Contents

Figures

About the Author

Emily M. Elliott, PhD., is a Professor of Psychology at Louisiana State University (LSU). Throughout her career she has studied the theoretical underpinnings of working memory and attention, as well as how attention and memory interact. She has also studied sounds that can be either helpful or hurtful to learning, depending on the situation, and the benefits of expertise afforded by musical training. She earned a BS in Psychology from LSU, an MA in Experimental Psychology and a PhD in Cognition and Neuroscience from the University of Missouri, Columbia. She began her faculty career as an Assistant Professor at LSU and was subsequently promoted to Associate Professor and then Full Professor. She is the Principal Investigator of the Elliott Attention Recall and Sounds (EARS) lab, training undergraduate and graduate students at LSU. She has written over 60 peer-reviewed publications and book chapters and is a Fellow of the Psychonomic Society and of Division 3 of the American Psychological Association.

Emily M. Elliott

About the Illustrator

Margaret "Maggie" M. Bagot is working towards a BS degree in Biological Sciences at LSU with a dual major in French. She has studied in France and intends to enroll in dental school. In her free time, she enjoys relaxing with friends, drawing and painting, and exercising.

Acknowledgements

I would like to thank Dayna Leaman for her positive attitude and her strong support throughout my career. She always told me that I should write a book one day, and this book would not have come about without her planting that seed.

I would also like to thank Jas Sullivan for his willingness to share his time and his overall patience and generosity as a colleague. He provided encouragement and support that helped me to jump into the water and start writing this book, even when I was not sure if I could do it.

Nelson Cowan was the greatest PhD advisor a person could ever ask for, and his steady commitment to research will always be remarkable to me. His contributions to the field over the years cannot be overstated. Thank you for helping me to become the researcher I am today.

Alan Strathman helped to start me on this path many years ago when he taught the Teaching of Psychology course at the University of Missouri in Columbia, Missouri. I had no idea how impactful that course would be, and I'd like to thank him for his patience and support. He introduced me to the concept of the pedagogy of teaching and helped me to see the classroom through a wider lens.

Thank you to Luke Elliott, Jr. for his extensive feedback on the full manuscript and his support on this project overall. Thanks also to Abby South and Elia Soto for their helpful comments and encouragement.

Part I

Setting the Foundation

Chapter 1

Introduction and Overview

Like many college students, I began my studies without knowing exactly what I wanted to do when I graduated. Also like many college students, I started in one major (Psychology), then added another (Theater) along the way to try to find my path. In my third year, I enrolled in a course on Human Memory. I do not recall having great expectations for this course, but it did seem interesting enough to be worth a try. I did not know that this course would change everything for me. Through that fall semester, I was exposed to the many puzzles that exist within the science of studying memory. I began to understand that it is a critical element of every person's life and defines who they are. Imagine your life with no memories of your past: simple things like which foods you prefer would not be so simple, not to mention complicated things like personal relationships. Studying memory helped me to see the complexities and challenges, as well as the very human and personal nature, of trying to design research protocols to unlock the mysteries of memory. I was hooked. From that point forward, I no longer wondered what my career would be. I dedicated myself to understanding human memory and cognition and I never did finish that Theater major. I made the decision to pursue a PhD on the most fascinating aspect of being human – memory.

The idea for this project has emerged over time and from many conversations with parents and families. As a researcher who studies school-aged children, I have interacted with numerous teachers, school leaders, and families over the years. The research that has been conducted in my laboratory has been at a basic level, with the goal of understanding the underlying mechanisms of memory and attention. However, there is a gap between the work in the lab and the daily life experiences of children in schools. There is also a gap in the published literature about children's memory and attention functioning. I believe that memory and attention are an important component of all lives, including children's. Once children reach school age, they begin to understand the need to remember information but are often not given strategies to improve their memories. This book provides concrete strategies with age-based tips and suggestions for supporting learning.

DOI: 10.4324/9781003672814-2

In addition, I have been asked several questions about attention, such as "What can I do to help my child/my student remain on task?" or "Is it really true that children's ability to pay attention is being harmed by current technology?". In the chapters that follow, I summarize current research and provide answers to these questions. Researchers have clearly demonstrated that the processes of attention, memory, and learning are closely linked. Many books, articles, or advice focus on one aspect of this interconnected relationship. There are very good books on attention and the role it can play in learning. There are very good books that focus on the strategies that can be deployed to improve memory and learning. What I would like to do in this book is to bring these topics together and discuss them as I feel they should be discussed – together! Memory and attention are incredibly interwoven and learning new material requires both systems. In the chapters that follow, I unpack and explain why it is important to think about memory and attention together.

There are also many myths about memory and how it works. I have heard them on children's programs and I have seen them in writing. How can professionals, who come from a wide range of training backgrounds, separate the facts and the fiction? How can parents, guardians, and teachers help children to be successful in applying their memory systems in daily life? This book also uncovers how current technology, including artificial intelligence (AI), is connected to our cognitive functioning; how to improve memory and attention; the amazing feats of memory that we perform every day; and the ways in which memory can be tricked. It also discusses why forgetting is not always a bad thing, and how we can maximize our performance on tasks involving memory and attention.

Why This Book?

Children are fascinating. As a researcher who studies memory and attention, I learned that one way to learn about memory was to study how it develops in children. Though I started from a scientific perspective, I quickly realized that children are funny and spontaneous and sometimes can really tax the patience of a research assistant. Nonetheless, working with them is a joy. Learning about how they learn and remember things, as well as how they deal with distractions, became a central part of my research. I want to share what I know with others and to help as many children as possible along the way.

This book is dedicated to helping professionals understand children's memory and attention systems and to helping children improve their memory functioning. It brings together my research and the research of others to synthesize and communicate with professionals, as well as with family members. My training as a cognitive psychologist with expertise in the development of memory and attention in children, and my years of working with children and families, gives me the background for translating research into everyday life.

Another motivation for writing this book comes from American data on the educational attainment of children. The US National Center for Education Statistics[1] has reported a decline in national standards for reading and mathematics in children aged between nine and 13. The most recent data available presents a sobering report of the largest declines in reading scores since 1990 and the first reported decline in math scores. The report from 2023[2] (the newest available at the time of writing) also showed a decline in reading and math scores. The report states: "Compared to a decade ago, the average scores declined seven points in reading and 14 points in mathematics". While there are likely multiple reasons for these challenges with academic achievement, children are not taught directly about their memory systems, or how to maximize their cognition by improving their understanding of memory and attention. This book is geared toward those who work with children and who may wish to learn about their own memory systems too.

The information in this book will be of interest to several types of reader. Several professionals, such as teachers, school administrators, mental health counselors, school counselors, and social workers, could apply the information to help children in schools. While books on the science of learning exist, the majority are written for professionals in higher education[3] who would apply the content to college students. There are few that target undergraduate students[4] as the audience and I have not seen any books that focus on memory and attention in children in the way this book does. Additionally, there is little work on the training that teachers receive on the concepts of memory and learning. Limited research has been conducted on teachers in the UK, and little to none exists on teachers in the US on these topics. It is important to understand teachers' awareness of concepts like the duration and capacity of working memory, as well as how to detect students in the classroom who may have a working memory deficit[5]. I talk more about working memory in a later chapter, but for now it is enough to know that it is a temporary storehouse of information that relates to tasks and thinking in the current moment. The UK research revealed a disconnect between the ability to identify children in the classroom who needed extra support and the appropriate strategies that could be used to help them. Furthermore, the findings from the UK survey are applicable to the context of classrooms in the US; demographic data reveals that the number of children with a learning disability has grown as well as the number of children who are learning English[6]. It is important for all children to succeed in education, regardless of their background, economic status, race/ethnicity, and disability status.

Reaching a broader audience of professionals, community members, and those in K-12 education will help to disseminate knowledge from the university context to the public. One reason this is important is to counteract myths about memory and learning that can be harmful, such as the myth of learning styles. This concept holds that a person has a narrow and specific modality of learning that is best for them, but also that they "cannot" learn effectively in a different modality. If a teacher emphasizes a written method of teaching a child who is an "auditory learner", then the child may believe that they cannot be successful because their learning style does not match the mode of delivery. There is no evidence of such learning styles, yet this myth is persistent, difficult to eradicate, and harmful to parents, teachers, and children[7]. I discuss this myth along with others that are potentially harmful to successful learning. Following this is a chapter on effective science-based strategies that facilitate learning. Thus, I move from myths to the current state of knowledge about memory and attention in action, with age-based guidance for children at different stages.

The book is written to be read as stand-alone chapters, if one has a particular interest in one or two topics, or as a full narrative. Throughout the book I include historical research to provide a perspective on where we have been as a field, and where we are going. Sometimes looking back at history can help us to understand the current situation, and this is also true for thinking about memory, attention, and how children learn. I also include the most recent research to illustrate the current state of knowledge in the field. I include stories and analogies to provide a context for thinking about scientific information and to make this book as accessible as possible. At the end of the book there is a glossary of terms, organized by chapter.

I am excited to take you on a journey with me. I want to share the knowledge I have gained and the fantastic experiences I have had as a researcher and as a college professor. It has been, and continues to be, a privilege to teach young people about their own cognition, memory, and attention. The students inspire me to keep learning, and to share what I know with as many others as possible. Happy reading!

Take-Away Points

- Memory and attention are interconnected. Thus, learning about one in isolation is not as helpful as learning about how these systems work together.
- Children have a great capacity to learn and there are many ways that the adults in their lives can support their learning.
- Myths about memory and attention are pervasive. This book provides easy-to-understand information about how memory and attention work and will help to dispel these myths.
- How memory and attention function together is discussed, followed by strategies from research on children's memory, attention, and learning.

Chapter Summary

I share the goal of maximizing children's learning potential. This book gives information about how the human memory and attention systems interact and develop in childhood. I want to strengthen our knowledge of memory and attention and minimize the potentially negative influence of myths. By starting with the basics of the interconnections of memory systems in the brain, and how to apply science-backed strategies at home, children and adults can be empowered to take charge of their learning. Given the rapid changes in technology, learning how to learn has never been more important.

Notes

1 National Center for Education Statistics provided the "NAEP Long-term trend assessment results: reading and mathematics". Retrieved from www.nationsreportcard.gov/highlights/ltt/2022/
2 National Center for Education Statistics provided the "NAEP Long-term trend assessment results: reading and mathematics". Retrieved from www.nationsreportcard.gov/highlights/ltt/2023/
3 Miller, M. D. (2022). *Remembering and forgetting in the age of technology: Teaching, learning, and the science of memory in a wired world.* West Virginia University Press.
4 Rhodes, M. G., Cleary, A. M. & DeLosh, E. L. (2020). *A guide to effective studying and learning: Practical strategies from the science of learning*. Oxford University Press.
5 Atkinson, A. L., Allen, R. J., & Waterman, A. H. (2021). Exploring the understanding and experience of working memory in teaching professionals: A large-sample questionnaire study. *Teaching and Teacher Education, 103,* 103343. https://doi.org/10.1016/j.tate.2021.103343
6 National Center for Education Statistics. NAEP Report Card: Reading. www.nationsreportcard.gov/reading/nation/groups/?grade=4
7 Sun X., Norton, O. & Nancekivell, S.E. (2023). Beware the myth: Learning styles affect parents', children's, and teachers' thinking about children's academic potential. *NPJ Science of Learning, 17,* 8(1):46. https://doi.org/10.1038/s41539-023-00190-x.

Chapter 2

The Basics

Understanding Neurons and Neuronal Networks

Many of you have seen images of brightly colored brains in news stories or other media. However, you may not know how we take in new information and how the anatomy of the brain supports new learning. This book is not intended to be a textbook of facts and figures about neuroanatomy; my goal is to provide information on how the brain works to help children maximize their memory and attention systems. The process starts with thinking about how learning happens within the brain. Learning causes changes in the structures of the brain itself, which is fascinating.

Neurons, Synapses, and Neurotransmitters

Neurons are the basic unit of the brain's anatomy. They are also sometimes called nerve cells. They help to send and receive information from other parts of the body and from the outside world. Neurons send messages to other neurons by a combination of electrical and chemical signals. The other cells in the brain, called glia cells, support and spread the signals from the neurons.

The number of neurons and neuronal connections is so vast that it is hard for most of us to grasp in concrete terms. I revisit this idea when I talk about the ability of our memory to store information over the long term. As is also discussed later in the book, there are several analogies to help us understand how the brain functions. A computer is one, and networks of different computers sharing information is another.

It is interesting that neurons do not actually touch each other. They communicate by sending neurotransmitters into the synapses, or the small spaces between neurons. The signaling process begins with the sending neuron (pre-synaptic neuron) releasing a neurotransmitter. The dendrites on the receiving neuron (post-synaptic neuron) propagate the signal (see Figure 2.1). The long part of the neuron, called the axon, is typically covered in a myelin sheath. This sheath serves as an "insulator" of sorts to protect the electrical signal as it travels from the cell body down the neuron's axon to the ending or terminal area of the neuron. The process continues by sending chemicals (neurotransmitters) into the synapse of the next neuron in the neuronal network.

DOI: 10.4324/9781003672814-3

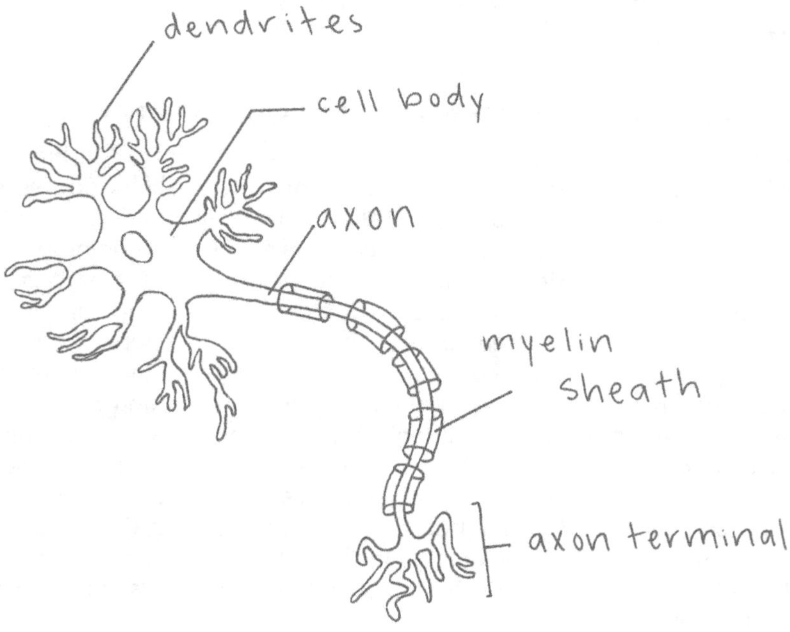

Figure 2.1 The different parts of the neuron: dendrites, cell body, axon, the axon covered in the myelin sheath and the axon terminal at the end of the neuron.

There are many important neurotransmitters that can be sent or received by one neuron to another. Neurons, synapses, and neurotransmitters make up networks of communication in the brain. Some neurons such as acetylcholine and dopamine are more important to learning and memory, while others such as serotonin are more important for mood regulation.

One way that understanding neurotransmitters can help us to maximize our function is by knowing which are the most relevant to particular behaviors, such as those supporting memory and attention. For example, research on the relationships between levels of neurotransmitters and the functioning of children with a diagnosis of Attention Deficit Hyperactivity Disorder (ADHD) is ongoing, and is changing our understanding of how stimulant medications affect brain function[1]. These medications are often prescribed to treat the symptoms of ADHD and were originally believed to improve attention itself. Newer research suggests that the parts of the brain responsible for processing rewards are affected (linked to the neurotransmitter dopamine) as well as areas responsible for wakefulness. The interpretation of these findings is that the children taking the medications are more interested in the tasks that they are working on and are also more alert as a result. I talk more about the interconnections of memory, attention, and ADHD in Chapter 5.

Areas of the Brain Important for Memory Functions

Neurons exist in networks in the cortex, or gray matter, of the brain. The word "cortex" comes from the Latin word for bark or shell and describes the wrinkled texture of the brain. As I discuss in more detail later, children and adults use the full range of brain areas in everyday functioning. Memory works through three widely recognized processes: encoding, storage, and retrieval. Encoding is the process of taking in details or noticing elements of the environment, and attention is an important component of successful encoding. For information to be retained over time, it must first be encoded into our systems. After successful encoding, neurons fire and new connections are forged to move information from encoding to storage. Ultimately, we need to retrieve the information that we have encoded and stored, so that we can use it when we need it. Retrieval is an active process, more complex than the analogy of pulling files from a file drawer might suggest. It takes communication between multiple areas of the brain to recreate the memory traces that constitute successful retrieval. Thus, multiple brain areas are involved in these three processes of memory.

However, it is also true that certain areas of the brain are better known for some functions than others. There are four lobes of the brain: the frontal, temporal, parietal, and occipital. Sitting at the back of the brain and above the brain stem is another structure called the cerebellum. It helps with movement, motor coordination, and posture. Research indicates that the cerebellum is also involved in multiple aspects of memory.

One way to think about this relates to the motor aspects of language. Speaking involves a motor plan that helps the brain to initialize the muscle movements that are needed. The cerebellum is involved in the motor movements of speech and is thus important in working memory. A fascinating fact about the cerebellum is that it contains 80 per cent of the neurons in the brain[2] and has many connections to multiple brain areas. However, the example of a motor plan and working memory involvement is just one way that the cerebellum plays a role in memory functions, and research is revealing more about the connections between the cortex and the cerebellum in our networked brains[3].

There are also two halves of the brain, or two hemispheres (see Figure 2.2). For example, the "left frontal region" is the front part of the brain on the left side. The hemispheres are used to control functioning on opposite sides of the body: the left hemisphere is involved in motor movements of the right side of the body, and vice versa. This is called contralateral function. I discuss lateralization of function in more detail in Chapter 8, including why it is not accurate to say that someone is "right-brained", for example.

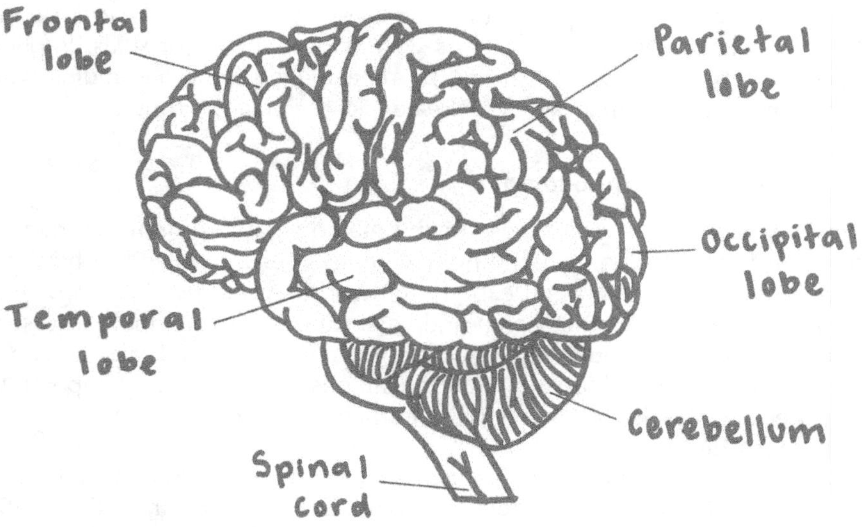

Figure 2.2 The left hemisphere of the brain including the four lobes, the cerebellum, and the brain stem leading to the spinal cord.

The portion of the brain that is critical for receiving visual information and translating it into signals that the brain can use for interpretation and action is known as the visual cortex. It is located at the back of the head in an area known as the occipital lobes.

The parietal lobes are situated above the occipital lobes and are important for body awareness and spatial knowledge. The parietal lobes help you to detect different sensations, such as knowing where your feet are located when you are sitting in a chair, even without looking at them.

The temporal lobes are located near the temples on both sides of the head. They are important for many aspects of auditory processing and language. Finally, the frontal lobes sit at the top and front area of the cortex and are vital for the motor movements of the body and regulating behavior. One area of the frontal lobes, the prefrontal cortex, is especially important for both memory and attention. Individuals with frontal lobe damage have difficulty inhibiting unacceptable behavior and with planning and decision making.

Although it is hard to describe a three-dimensional structure like the brain this way, I think of the "medial" or middle part of the brain as sitting behind the temporal lobes. Within the cortex there are important structures for learning and memory, such as the hippocampus and the amygdala. The amygdala plays a major role in emotional processing, and memories and emotions can be closely linked. A specific type of learning known as fear conditioning is linked to the amygdala and is thought to be a type of implicit memory. I discuss this in more detail in Chapter 4, but for now, it is enough to know that implicit memories can support quick access to the meanings of words below the level of conscious awareness, as well as other habits or skills. Implicit memory can also support learning by repeatedly pairing a stimulus with something such as a mild shock to create a learned fear response.

The Role of the Hippocampus

The hippocampus is critical for moving memories into a more permanent form, or long-term storage. The hippocampus is also involved in how we take in new information and explore the world around us[4]. We know this from both experimental research and case studies of individuals who sustained damage or underwent surgery that affected their brain function. Without an intact and functional hippocampus, it is practically impossible to experience life in the moment and to then store those moments as long-term memories.

Our original understanding of the hippocampus and its role in the formation of long-term memories occurred by accident. A case from the 1950s was a man who suffered very severe seizures caused by epilepsy. Medicine to control the seizures was not effective and he was unable to live an independent life. When he was 27 years old, he underwent a surgical procedure to remove parts of his brain to try to control the seizure activity. The surgery successfully reduced the seizures but it did not eliminate them. It also had the dramatic side effect of creating a form of amnesia known as anterograde amnesia, which is characterized by the loss of the ability to form new memories. His perceptual and working memory systems were intact; however, he was unable to transfer his short-term experiences into long-term memories. He was known to the scientific community as H. M. After his death in 2008, his name was revealed as Henry Molaison. It was striking to learn that one of the major discoveries regarding how memories were created in the brain came from surgery that had nothing to do with memory itself.

Mr. Molaison participated in research studies that helped scientists to understand the specific areas of the brain that were removed during the surgery, as well as which aspects of his cognitive functioning were preserved and which were impaired[5]. Over decades of interviews, researchers learned that he was an intelligent man with a sense of humor even though he had no ability to form new long-term memories. Through these studies, Mr Molaison's case revealed that some types of memory can be preserved in an extreme case like his, even though most of his experiences post-surgery were never retained. Thus, the hippocampus became recognized as a central structure in the retention of memories over time.

The Role of Emotions

Another example of the importance of the hippocampus is the sudden memory that springs to mind when you encounter a familiar smell. It can transport you back in time to a much earlier memory, such as coming home and smelling your favorite meal cooking on the stove. The sudden retrieval of a memory based upon a cue from a smell has to do with the way that our brains are structured. The sense of smell has a more direct pathway to the amygdala, an area of the brain responsible for helping us to experience and process emotions, than the other senses (sight, sound, taste, and touch), which are routed through the thalamus first. The thalamus is a structure in the midbrain that functions as a relay station for input from the other senses. However, smells have more direct access to structures in the midbrain like the amygdala and the hippocampus. When the sense of smell is associated with emotions, such as the positive feelings of arriving home, a link is created between the smell and the good feelings. This link enables the retrieval cue of the smell to bring back the emotions and the memory related to the smell.

Scientists believe that the unique pathway in the brain related to smells, emotions, and memories has evolutionary importance. Thus, understanding the relationship among smells, emotions, and memories gives us another way to capitalize on our memory system and how it functions. Not every smell-related memory is positive, and not every smell-related memory is necessarily a strong emotional memory[6]. Nonetheless, smells, emotions, and memories often are experienced together in our lives.

Areas of the Brain Important for Attention Functions

Just as there are multiple brain areas that support memory through the different stages of encoding, storage, and retrieval, there are multiple areas of the brain that support the different functions of attention. As mentioned above, the front area of the brain that is located behind your forehead is called the frontal lobes. One part of the frontal lobes is the prefrontal cortex, and it is linked with many of the processes that are involved in attention. We need the prefrontal cortex to direct our attention and to avoid distractions from stimuli or information that is not relevant to the task we are trying to complete. In addition, there are networks connecting the prefrontal cortex and the parietal lobes, which are located on the top of the head, above the occipital lobes.

Evidence from patients who have damage to the parietal lobes indicates that there is a disconnect between their ability to take in a new stimulus and then pay attention to it. The patients do not have any damage to their visual system or their ability to process new information visually. However, they are often unable to indicate what they saw, specifically on only one side. The one-sided nature of this gap in their awareness, known as "contralateral neglect", is associated with the hemisphere that contains the lesion (remember that the brain hemispheres control the opposite side of the body). Patients with damage to the parietal area of the right hemisphere show evidence of problems or gaps when reporting objects on their left side. This is evidence of the role of the parietal lobes in attentional functions. While this has been observed in some children as well[7], it is rare and is more often associated with adults who have suffered some type of brain injury, such as a stroke.

Reconstructive Nature of Memory

The neurons and synapses discussed above are involved in creating patterns of neuronal firing that can trigger several actions. The neurons fire very rapidly, which sends neurotransmitters across the synapse and into receiving cells. The networks of neurons that make up your memories communicate with each other to recreate the experiences you have had. One analogy is that networks of neurons are similar to trees and their large root systems (see Figure 2.3). These networks function in different parts of the brain and can help to recreate specific parts of the memory, such as the way something smelled, the way something looked, or how you felt at the time. Each memory is really rebuilding the details as opposed to playing back an exact replication of the event. This is what I meant when I described the process of retrieval as active. Unlike what you may have seen in a video or a movie, memory does not work by replaying an exact copy of something that you have already experienced. There is no rewind button in the brain. I return to this concept in Chapter 9 when I talk about the active nature of retrieval practice as an effective strategy for learning.

Brain Development in Children

Studying brain development in children gives important insights into the amazing learning systems that humans have evolved over time. The cognitive and developmental psychologist Jean Piaget called children "little scientists" because they are constantly taking in new information and adapting to it in their environments. Neural evidence of this comes from research that examined the cognitive capabilities of young children and how the growing brain changes in response to their interactions, conversations, and other sources of input. As one example, babies are born with the ability to hear and recognize every sound in the human language, regardless of where they are born or the native language of their mothers[8]. Over time, however, the brain "cleans itself up" through a process of neuronal pruning that eliminates neuronal

Figure 2.3 **Connectedness among neurons and neuronal networks, highlighting the analogy with trees with interconnected roots.**

connections that are not used to make room for new learning. Continued exposure to the language of the home environment helps the brain to tune the system to the sounds of baby's language. By around one year old, babies are no longer able to distinguish sounds in new languages in the same way that they did at birth[9]. This ability to change in response to input from the environment is known as "plasticity".

The plasticity and resilience of the human brain are remarkable. This is especially true in children. Learning how the brain can rewire itself in the event of damage or injury shows us how it is so much more than just a machine. Case studies provide examples of complete restructuring of brain systems that typically perform specific functions. Children who are born without vision, for example, develop advanced hearing abilities[10] and the areas of the brain typically devoted to processing visual stimuli can be recruited to assist in other tasks. Studies have shown that parts of the occipital cortex become involved in the processing of sounds and tactile (or touch) stimuli in those born without vision or who suffer lesions to the brain in early life, often as the result of a stroke or other form of brain injury[11].

Take-Away Points

- The building blocks of brain function are neurons, synapses, and the interconnected neuronal networks.
- The brain communicates both electrically and chemically; neurotransmitters that are important for memory are acetylcholine and dopamine.
- Two important structures for memory and emotion are the hippocampus and the amygdala.
- Children's brains develop rapidly and enable new learning at a remarkable pace, yet it does take time and experience to create large and interconnected networks in the brain.
- Learning occurs through plasticity, or the ability of the brain to create new neuronal connections and change in response to experiences.

Chapter Summary

The brain is part of a system that takes in new information through the senses, processes it, consolidates it, and allows you to create both immediate and long-term memories. At a basic level, neurons are the essence of the nervous system that allow the brain and spinal cord to communicate with the rest of the body. Neurons are the smallest part of the neuronal networks that communicate with each other and create patterns of firing that lead to memories. Neurons send signals across the synapses. Two neurotransmitters that are particularly important to learning and memory are acetylcholine and dopamine. There are also areas of the brain that are critical to memory functioning, such as the temporal lobes and the hippocampus. Damage to these areas of the brain from brain injury, strokes, or other forms of head trauma can result in impaired memory. Attentional functions are supported by structures in the frontal and parietal lobes. Our brains are interconnected systems that communicate across multiple brain regions to rebuild and reconstruct our memories in real time. Brain plasticity is important for learning to take place throughout life, because the brain can change in response to input from the environment.

Notes

1 Ballard, S. (2025). Stimulant ADHD medications work differently than thought. WashU Medicine. https://medicine.washu.edu/news/stimulant-adhd-medications-work-differently-than-thought/
2 Prati, J. M., Pontes-Silva, A., & Gianlorenço, A. C. L. (2024). The cerebellum and its connections to other brain structures involved in motor and non-motor

functions: A comprehensive review. *Behavioural Brain Research, 465,* 114933. https://doi.org/10.1016/j.bbr.2024.114933

3 Song, B., Tian, M., Wang, T., Wang, X., Ye, X., Yao, Q., ... & Yin, K. (2025). Effects of cerebellar repetitive transcranial magnetic stimulation at different frequencies on working memory: An EEG study. *CNS Neuroscience & Therapeutics, 31*(7), e70491.

4 Lucas, H. D., Duff, M. C., & Cohen, N. J. (2019). The hippocampus promotes effective saccadic information gathering in humans. *Journal of Cognitive Neuroscience,* 31(2), 186–201. https://doi.org/10.1162/jocn_a_01336

5 Augustinack, J. C., Van der Kouwe, A. J., Salat, D. H., Benner, T., Stevens, A. A., Annese, J., ... & Corkin, S. (2014). HM's contributions to neuroscience: A review and autopsy studies. *Hippocampus, 24*(11), 1267–1286. https://doi.org/10.1002/hipo.22354

6 Bogenschütz, L., Bermeitinger, C., Brörken, A., Schlüter, H., & Hackländer, R. P. (2022). Odor-associated memories are not necessarily highly emotional. *Acta Psychologica, 230,* 103767.

7 Trauner, D. A. (2003). Hemispatial neglect in young children with early unilateral brain damage. *Developmental Medicine and Child Neurology, 45*(3), 160–166. https://doi.org/10.1111/j.1469-8749.2003.tb00924.x

8 Golinkoff, R. M., & Hirsh-Pasek, K. (2000). *How babies talk: The magic and mystery of language in the first three years of life.* Penguin.

9 Thompson, R. A. (2023). *The brain development revolution: Science, the media, and public policy.* Cambridge University Press.

10 Dhondekar, I., & Vanaja, C. S. (2024). Auditory processing abilities of children with congenital blindness. *International Journal of Pediatric Otorhinolaryngology, 186,* 112126. https://doi.org/10.1016/j.ijporl.2024.112126

11 Marins, T. F., Russo, M., Rodrigues, E. C., Monteiro, M., Moll, J., Felix, D., ... & Tovar-Moll, F. (2023). Reorganization of thalamocortical connections in congenitally blind humans. *Human Brain Mapping, 44*(5), 2039–2049. https://doi.org/10.1002/hbm.26192

Chapter 3

Analogies to Explain Memory

A common theme across humanity is wanting to understand how things work. As history has shown, curiosity drives innovation and can lead to creative solutions to problems. From the very early philosophers and ancient Greeks, people have written about the mind and the capacity of memory. As we strive to understand the world around us, we often rely on analogies as a means of clarifying concepts, making connections, and illustrating the causal relationships that exist. Memory is no exception.

Technology as a Medium for Analogies

As society has changed, the analogies to describe memory changed as well[1]. The earliest references to the mind and to memory came from Aristotle and Plato. They made comparisons to using a wax seal or wax tablet, so that a person could "make an impression" that would be stored in the wax itself. Additionally, the descriptions of memory and memory processes are linked to the idea that we can take in information and "place it" within the mind. Thinking about retrieving a memory is often described as "finding the memory", which may be hidden "deep within the brain". The way that people think about their memories is reflected in how early psychologists such as William James talked about memory as though it were a house with many rooms. You may have also heard of the idea of a "memory palace"[2]. These metaphors help our understanding of memory, but can also contribute to myths or misunderstandings if someone takes the analogy too literally. Using spatial language or metaphors for the single location of a memory in the brain does not fit the concepts of neuronal networks and reconstructive nature of memory discussed in Chapter 2, but it is sometimes a useful way to describe the experience of retrieving a memory.

The use of technology analogies to explain memory moved from a wax tablet in the ancient days to a more modern analogy like the gramophone in the mid-20th century[3]. The analogies changed again when people transitioned from listening to radio programs to watching television shows, and then again when recording devices became common and video cassette recorders could

DOI: 10.4324/9781003672814-4

play back entire programs. However, as discussed in Chapter 2, each time we remember an event in our lives or try to recall a fact, we are **rebuilding** the experience, not replaying the exact copy of the prior scene. Knowing that memory is reconstructive is important because it helps us to understand why you need good cues to be able to rebuild the context and retrieve the details. The more cues you have to recall information, the more traces you can follow to reinstate the missing pieces.

As computer technology became more common and more households had access to computers, analogies comparing short-term memory to random access memory (RAM) and long-term memory to a computer hard drive were used. Technology supplied these comparisons because many people began to understand the idea that holding something briefly in mind (like in short-term memory) is different from saving a file more permanently, such as to the hard drive of a computer. I discuss short-term and long-term memory in more detail in Chapter 4.

Comparisons Between Human Memory and Artificial Intelligence

It is important to understand that the brain consists of neural networks that connect different elements of memories. These networks can be recombined through retrieval into one coherent memory, and the same combination is not used every single time a memory is retrieved. This knowledge sets the stage for a discussion of the analogy between human memory and AI. Does AI behave like human memory? A technical answer to this question is beyond the scope of this book. Some experts agree that AI was informed by knowledge of the functioning of the human brain, while others say that the capacity of the human brain is far superior to any machine. Nonetheless, there are similarities between the ways that models of AI and human memory both rely upon prior knowledge and analysis of patterns. Both systems also use networks of information, and the ability of current large language models (LLMs) to produce outputs emerged when computer scientists and engineers used the concept of neurons with connections to create early artificial neural networks[3].

Around the 1950s, psychologists and computer scientists began to ask questions about human cognition and our ability to build machines that could do calculations. These questions led to the emergence of both Cognitive Psychology as a discipline and AI as a concept. Tony Prescott, Professor of Cognitive Robotics and the author of *The Psychology of Artificial Intelligence,* describes a summer workshop that was held at Dartmouth in 1956. The organizer, an academic named John McCarthy, proposed the term "AI" as the title of this workshop to capture the concept of "smart machines". Thus, he is credited with the first use of the term.

Progress in research in both computing and cognitive psychology continued in the 1960s and 1970s, and scientists predicted that computers would be able to learn without being programmed. Scientists from different fields began to influence the evolution of computing through their investigations into how the brain works, aided by the interdisciplinary fields of cognitive science and cognitive neuroscience. Thus, the first successes in AI development came from attempts to create a computer model based upon the architecture of the human brain.

While generative AI tools, often called Gen AI for short, regularly make news, the use of different technologies in the classroom to enhance learning outcomes is not new. I think of AI as an umbrella term that encompasses different types of technology. Some have been around for a long time, and we have become used to examples like simple chatbots and automated phone-answering services that process spoken human language and direct calls. However, every time someone says "AI" they may not mean Gen AI. Given the rapid pace of development of so many new tools to automate and facilitate our learning and our workflows, it is important for people to use specific language when talking about the AI tools that are being used. It is also very important to think about how these technologies are being implemented in classrooms.

Artificial Intelligence Tools in the Classroom

In 2013 researchers studied the use of learning tools called "intelligent tutors" in math instruction[4]. The intelligent tutors were adaptive to the individual learner, interactive, and computer based. These tools could provide hints or other types of feedback to support learning, based on the needs of the individual student. The researchers reviewed work published between 1997 and 2010 and included 26 studies in their meta-analysis (a comprehensive search of published articles and examination of the outcomes of multiple studies).

Interestingly, some of the questions that were being asked then are still relevant today in educational technology. How do learning outcomes differ between human instruction and intelligent tutoring systems? How will different children benefit from the use of these tools? Will all children show equal benefit, or will some benefit more than others? The conclusions of the 2013 meta-analysis found no negative effects of intelligent tutoring systems; the positive effects were evident but small. The benefits were better for the general range of students than for those students who were lower in achievement levels. Given the improvements in technology and the major changes in AI models regarding individualization and responsiveness to student feedback, it is important to continue to ask these questions and to think about how best to benefit all learners of all types.

Given the proliferation of new AI tools, the research in this area is also developing rapidly. A 2025 meta-analysis of learning technologies examined the interaction of different types of AI tools in four main domains: cognitive, knowledge utilization, metacognition, and psychological functioning[5]. I discuss metacognitive processes in more detail in Chapter 7, where I also discuss metamemory. The type of work that was reviewed in the 2013 meta-analysis can now be greatly expanded and can include a much broader range of educational technology. The 2025 authors included 228 peer-reviewed publications in their meta-analysis, as opposed to the 26 in the earlier one. The findings indicated that more papers focused on cognitive outcomes than on metacognitive outcomes. Examples of the AI tools in these studies are Gen AI tools, intelligent tutoring, chatbots, and intelligent robots. Overall, LLMs and Gen AI tools were found to be the most effective tools for improving cognitive outcomes. The newer versions of the technology made greater gains than what had been reported in the 2013 meta-analysis, which is not surprising given how much these models have evolved.

The 2025 meta-analysis also raised several important issues. For example, there are now products that help to create custom and individualized math lessons; while these are promising, more work is needed. One point of view is that the use of AI tools in the classroom will become even more relevant as the nation-wide teacher shortage in the US continues. It remains to be seen if parents and caregivers will respond positively to the idea that AI tools could replace human teachers. Additionally, issues related to access must be considered. Differences in the social and economic status of different school systems will mean different levels of access to AI tools. Given the high cost of some of the most advanced tools, we could be facing a new challenge of providing access to all students, regardless of which country or school district they live.

An important related question is how models of AI can be trained, and how that process does or does not compare to the ways in which children learn. Developmental psychologist Alison Gopnik and her colleagues are conducting research into how children learn, abstract new details and generalize from the world in comparison to the limits of some AI models[6].

One of Dr Gopnik's lines of research investigated multiple models of AI, including ChatGPT 4, which had been trained using both text and images. Chat GPT performed better than other AI models that had only been trained on text. Nonetheless, presenting children and AI models with situations requiring problem solving indicated that the children could outperform the AI models. One example asked some children from three to seven years old and the models to select a tool for drawing a circle. The children understood that using something round would help them, such as a tea kettle, even if it was not designed for drawing a circle. The computer models did not perform as well. This outcome suggests that innovation is a skill that even young children possess, and that this skill is different from imitation.

An LLM is very good at imitating the style of other writers and can generate new word combinations using the correct syntax. However, a limitation of the current systems is seen when true innovation is required. The authors discuss the emergence of tool use as a sign of intelligent behavior in multiple species and question whether any AI systems have this capability.

At the time of writing, AI tools are providing new solutions, new adaptations, and new interfaces to everyday life. Keeping up with the rapid pace of development and change in this field can seem overwhelming. The addition of "multimodal" AI tools, such as those that can incorporate images or live camera feeds as well as auditory information such as recordings or environmental sounds, have enhanced the options of what AI tools can provide. In this way, the developers are extending the analogy of the human information processing system and the way we take in information through our senses to expand the capabilities of AI tools. Human memory and AI tools continue to influence each other, and the pace of change is very rapid. While it is helpful at some level to think of our brains as machines, much is still unknown about our brains and their complex functions. The brain's plasticity, or how it changes in response to the environment[7], tells us there is still much to learn about the complex interactions of the multiple brain areas with each other and with our bodies. While the brain shows plasticity, AI tools cannot cope with a loss of function in the same way that a human brain can.

Is New Technology Necessarily a Bad Thing?

New technology is often seen as a threat to good brain function, but is that true? When a new technology is widely embraced, there are often concerns that the way we think, or learn, or even interact with other people, will be negatively affected. Just as the analogies of memory have changed over time, concerns about memory and attention being negatively affected by new technology are not new. Despite these concerns, we continue to see human innovation, new solutions to problems, and other evidence of technological improvements. Children are no exception and are adapting in new and creative ways to the learning tools that are available to them. Research continues to inform teachers, parents, and other caregivers about the possible integration of AI in the classroom and beyond.

Take-Away Points

- Analogies to explain memory have been around for over 2000 years and evolve as technology changes.
- The fields of cognitive psychology and the study of AI emerged around the same time in the mid-1950s.
- Computer analogies are commonly used to explain memory, and the current AI models are based upon neuronal networks in the brain. Yet our brains are more sophisticated than any computer.

- Research with children and AI has shown that children are more innovative than these models and can go beyond imitation to learn new things; however, the AI models are changing rapidly and it is important to monitor new advancements.

Chapter Summary

Analogies are a useful tool to deepen understanding of a concept. Analogies to explain human memory, how it functions, and how it is structured have been around for centuries. As technology has changed, so have the analogies that have been drawn. The current analogies regarding computers have helped to develop our understanding of both computing and human memory. Scientists and researchers have used the ability of the human brain to make predictions when learning new information to develop LLMs and AI tools. In turn, the field's understanding of how to maximize memory performance is improving. Children play an important role in helping us to understand how best to use these technologies to enhance learning.

Notes

1 Roediger, H.L. (1980). Memory metaphors in cognitive psychology. *Memory & Cognition 8,* 231–246. https://doi.org/10.3758/BF03197611
2 Foer, J. (2011). *Moonwalking with Einstein: The art and science of remembering everything*. Penguin.
3 Prescott, T. (2025). *The psychology of AI*. Routledge.
4 Steenbergen-Hu, S. & Cooper, H. (2013). A meta-analysis of the effectiveness of intelligent tutoring systems on K–12 students' mathematical learning. *Journal of Educational Psychology, 105*(4), 970–987. https://doi.org/10.1037/a0032447
5 Yeo, G. & Lansford, J. E. (2025). Effects of Artificial Intelligence on educational functioning: A review and meta-analysis. *Educational Psychology Review, 37*(4), 110. https://doi.org/10.1007/s10648-025-10085-5
6 Yiu, E., Kosoy, E., & Gopnik, A. (2024). Transmission versus truth, imitation versus innovation: What children can do that large language and language-and-vision models cannot (yet). *Perspectives on Psychological Science, 19*(5), 874–883. https://doi.org/10.1177/17456916231201401
7 Kirby, E. D., Glenn, M. J., Sandstrom, N. J., & Williams, C. L. (2024). *Introduction to behavioral neuroscience*. OpenStax. https://openstax.org/books/introduction-behavioral-neuroscience/pages/1-introduction

Part II

Digging Deeper

How Do We Learn, Remember, and Forget?

Chapter 4

The Differences between Short-term, Working, and Long-term Memory

People commonly use the terms "short-term" and "long-term" memory. These are time-based distinctions that make sense to us, because we know that remembering something we did very recently is different than remembering something we did weeks or even years ago.

To cognitive psychologists, short-term memory is **very** short and really means the moment-to-moment parts of your life, such as what you are doing right now, what you are thinking about right now, or what you are planning to grab when you walk into the kitchen, right now. Because of this, we think of short-term memory as lasting about 30 seconds[1]. On the other hand, if it is the evening and you are thinking about what you had for breakfast that day, we consider that long-term memory. Dividing it up this way is based upon research on people who have injuries or damage to their brains. I discuss Henry Molaison in Chapter 2 as an extreme example of a patient who no longer had his hippocampus. Such cases have shown that we have a very small amount of time to take in new things from the environment and process them in our brains before the information is lost. By defining different tasks based on the time between when new information is presented and the time that the information is needed again, cognitive psychologists have tried to understand both the structure and the function of our memory systems.

Sensory Memory

Before going into more detail about short-term memory, it is important to start with a type of memory that many people may not even know about: sensory memory. The reason that most people are not aware of type of memory is that it has an extremely brief duration (one to four seconds). However, it is critically important in taking in information from the environment and helping us to determine which details we want to focus on and process more deeply. Each sense has a sensory memory associated with it. Researchers know the most about visual (or iconic) and auditory (echoic) sensory memory. However, scientists have also studied sensory memories associated with touch, or tactile sensory memory, and odor, or the sensory memory associated with olfaction.

DOI: 10.4324/9781003672814-6

Visual and auditory sensory memory seem to operate behind the scenes, but it makes our experience of seeing and listening in the world much more seamless. As we take in information, our eyes are constantly making small movements, or saccades. These small movements prevent any one area of the eye from getting too fatigued by constantly firing. They are often so small that even if you are looking directly at someone, you do not notice them. However, our experience of vision is smooth and connected. We do not experience any gaps or blurs when our eyes make a movement from one location to another. This smoothness of perception is the result of visual sensory memory. It has a duration of approximately one second, and often the information in visual sensory memory is replaced by new information as we continue to look around and take in the world.

Our auditory sensory memories also help us to fill in the gaps, but the duration is longer than visual sensory memory. The duration of auditory sensory memory can be as long as four seconds. This is logical given that sounds unfold over time, while vision can support the perception of multiple items simultaneously. Sometimes, when you are deep in a book, someone comes into the room and asks you a question. You immediately ask them to repeat it, but upon a moment's reflection, you realize you do know what they said, and you can almost replay the sounds in your mind. This ability to store and repeat auditory information over the course of a few seconds is known as auditory sensory memory and it helps us to process sounds in our environment and determine which ones we want to focus on for deeper processing. The duration is not long enough to bring back an entire conversation, but it does help to fill in small gaps in time.

Short-Term Memory

Because there are so many different sights and sounds in our environment, we need the combination of sensory memory, attention, short-term memory, and finally working memory and long-term memory to function in our daily lives. Sensory memory is often described as a gatekeeper of information. Whether or not information will make it into short-term or working memory for deeper processing can depend upon several factors. Once information is selected for further processing, it is likely that it will move into short-term memory. As mentioned above, short-term memory has a longer duration than sensory memory, up to about 30 seconds. But the capacity of short-term memory is smaller than that of sensory memory, which indicates that we can only accommodate a certain amount in our cognitive systems.

One way that we have studied short-term memory in children is using a task called a memory span task. Scientists and clinicians wanted to understand the limits to the number of items a person can hold in their mind at one time without making any mistakes. Research in this area was first conducted in the late 1880s by Ebbinghaus[2] and Jacobs[3]. For example,

I might give you a list of three numbers and ask you to tell them back to me in order. Then, if you can do that, I increase to four numbers and ask you to tell them back to me in order. This process continues until you are no longer able to tell me the numbers in the correct order. At that point, I know that you have hit the limit, or "span", of numbers that you can remember in order. This task is conducted with a focus on memory in an immediate sense and participants are not allowed to use any devices or to write anything down. It is all based upon what they can retain in their own minds for a short period.

Being a participant in a memory span task can be frustrating because the researchers are literally pushing you to the point of making mistakes; however, this is very informative. If participants performed perfectly on every trial, it would be very hard for us to discover what factors lead to better or worse performance. It is necessary to push people to the point of making mistakes so that we can learn why they are happening. Memory span research has been important in building our understanding of developmental changes in memory in children as well as individual differences in adults.

As one example of the research conducted in my lab, my colleagues and I did a very large study on short-term memory span in children[4]. It was important to us to learn more about how children remember information in order, and whether this ability was the same in different countries. Because children may start going to school at different ages in different countries, we wondered if that starting age had any effect on how many things a child can remember. In our study, we worked with children who were five, six, seven, and ten years old. We asked them to remember a series of pictures that were shown on a computer screen. We started by only asking them to remember two pictures, in order. Then we gradually increased to a total of five pictures that had to be recalled in the correct order to be counted as a correct response.

What we learned is that younger children can remember fewer items in order than older children. We also learned that the country the children lived in did not have any effect on the number of pictures that they could remember, whether the US, the UK, Germany, or Costa Rica (to name a few). This limit is an important detail to understand, especially when giving someone a set of tasks to do, or instructions for a school assignment. Remembering the information in order is a more complex task than recalling the items in any order. By the time the children are ten years old, they are much more likely to be able to retain four or five items in order. This difference in memory span abilities by age group helps us to understand that if a five-year-old child is told to complete a four-step instruction list, it is very possible that not all those steps will remain in their short-term memory. On the other hand, a ten-year-old child would find this task much easier.

The implications of this research are clear for the classroom and for the home environment. Sometimes it may seem like a child is not listening or not following directions; yet maybe they are trying. It could be the case that the number of instructions is more than they can remember at one time. It is important to create instructions, especially multi-step instructions, that take the memory limits and ages of children into account.

Working Memory

Short-term memory is very important in many tasks, such as learning new words or phone numbers. Often, though, we do more than just repeat something to ourselves and then immediately try to remember it. When we have information in our mind and need to use it for something we are doing, cognitive psychologists call this "working memory"[5]. If you have ever tried to solve a two-digit addition problem in your head, like 15 + 29 =?, you are using your working memory (see Figure 4.1). You must complete the first addition (5 + 9 = 14) and then hold onto that part of the answer while doing the rest of the problem (carry the one, 2 + 1 = 3 +1 = 4; the total answer is 44). This "working" aspect of the things you hold in your mind makes it a working memory situation, and a bit different from a short-term memory situation that only involves simple repetition of items until you no longer need them.

Working memory is important for children's schoolwork and is used when reading, working on math problems, learning new vocabulary, and many other tasks. It is helpful to know that even though we can only keep a limited number of things in our working memory, just like short-term memory, we can use strategies to help us to learn new things. I talk more about strategies in Chapter 9, but to give a quick example: breaking down complicated sets of information into smaller steps makes it easier to remember, and then it is more likely that the outcome will be correct. Grouping a longer list into subsets of shorter lists is known as chunking. If a long recipe is broken down into a description of what to do with the dry ingredients, what to do with the wet ingredients, and then what to do once everything is combined, it is easier to follow than if everything were laid out as single steps and individual processes. It creates less of a load on the working memory system, and it also makes it easier to update working memory by making it easier to determine if a step has already been completed.

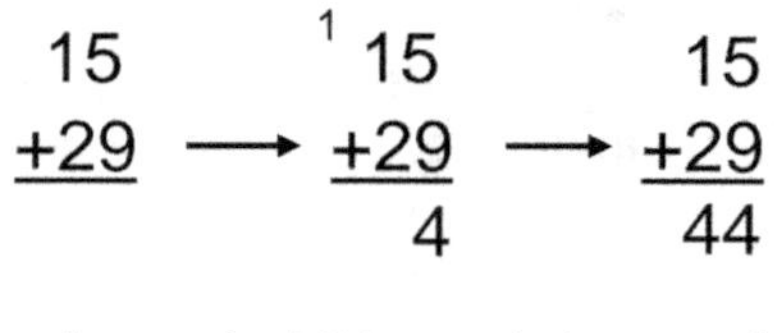

Figure 4.1 The process of mental addition and the use of working memory. The intermediate step must be held in mind to get to the final answer in the math problem.

Similar to age-related changes in the capacity of short-term memory, research has indicated clear changes in the capacity of working memory as children grow. Working memory tasks are different than the short-term memory span task described above in that they typically contain an extra component. Short-term memory tasks often involve the immediate presentation and retention of a series of items. Working memory tasks commonly include more processing, as opposed to simply being able to focus on the items to be remembered and to report them back, in order[6]. Working memory tests may ask a child to complete a task in between the presentation of the items that are to be remembered. An example is presenting a set of three letters to be remembered, in order. However, between presenting each letter, the experimenters also ask the child to solve an easy math problem, such as, "Does 1 + 1 = 2?" (see Figure 4.2).

The inclusion of a secondary task is designed to make the child switch their attentional focus between the two tasks. In this way, the working memory span tasks are designed to tax the cognitive system and to present distractions from the main goal. These tasks are a slightly more realistic assessment of immediate memory in daily life, because we are very often interrupted while doing a task. Research has shown that younger children, around five to six years of age, can only remember two or three items when doing a complex

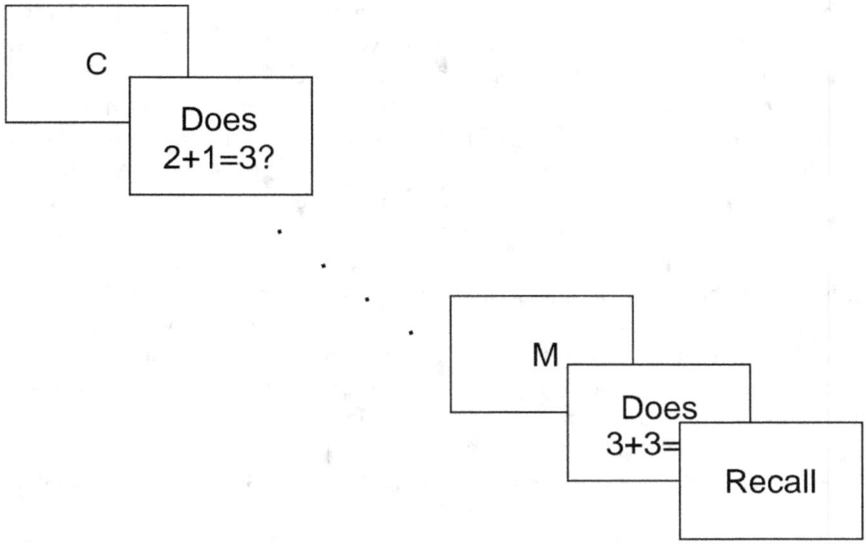

Figure 4.2 Task design in a complex span task used to measure working memory capacity in children using different screens. They include a letter to be remembered on one screen, followed by a math problem to be solved. The recall screen prompts recall of only the letters.

working memory span task. This working memory span capacity increases with age, so by 11 to 12 years of age the capacity is similar to young adults and reaches four, plus or minus one item.

Long-Term Memory

When a person remembers something special that happened in their life, such as a birthday party, that is what cognitive psychologists call "long-term memory". Research has shown that people can remember very large amounts of information from many years ago. It is possible that long-term memory has no capacity limits; your brain can hold so much information that it will not "get full"[7].

Long-term memory can be thought about in two different ways: the kind of memory you use when doing something with your muscles and your body, like playing tennis, and the kind of memory you use when remembering something with words or that you could talk about to someone else[8]. Sometimes people talk about "muscle memory", which I think is what cognitive psychologists call "**procedural memory**". It is the kind of memory you use when riding a bike, kicking a soccer ball, or playing a musical instrument. It comes from a lot of practice and can be hard to describe to someone else. It is much easier to teach someone to ride a bicycle by having them hop on the bike than it is to try to explain it to them in words. Procedural memories help us to perform lots of tasks that involve the movement of our bodies. **Declarative** memories are made up of the experiences we have had and the facts that we know, and these are much easier to talk about and describe in words.

As discussed in Chapter 2, the brain works by making connections between ideas or concepts. If you already know something about a topic, like the differences between an alligator and a crocodile, it can be easier for you to learn related things (like the differences between a turtle and a tortoise). Your working memory can use information that you have in your long-term memory to make connections and come up with new ways to think about something. This process helps us to understand why analogies can be a good thing; if you are having trouble understanding something new when it is told to you in one way, having another way to think about it may make it easier. An analogy can help you compare something in your long-term memory to something new. If you are learning a new move in your martial arts class, the instructor might compare it to something you know, like a frog jump. This comparison makes it easier to understand the new movement and makes it easier to remember as well.

Our long-term memories are of different kinds: the memories from our own life (like a birthday), called **episodic** memories, and the memory of facts (like Baton Rouge is the capital city of Louisiana), called **semantic** memories (see

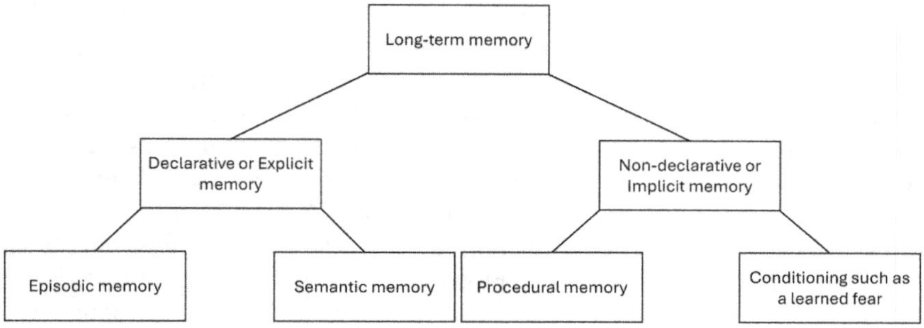

Figure 4.3 **Hierarchical structure of the long-term memory system to illustrate the organization of different subtypes.**

Figure 4.3). We know this from people who have had damage to their brains from some kind of injury or accident[9].

We do not need to know where we were when we first learned the capital city of Louisiana, but we need to know that fact. Semantic memories help us to remember facts (who was the first President of the US?) and episodic memories help us to remember who we are and the things we have done in our lives.

Highly Superior Autobiographical Memories in Children

Episodic memory is often described as the personal view of experiences and "episodes" from someone's life. Sometimes these episodes can be shared with others. A child or adult can imagine how other people felt about and experienced the same events. However, there is a type of memory that is unique to each one of us, called **autobiographical** memory. Just as a biography is a story of someone's life told by someone else, and an autobiography is the story of someone's life told by that person, autobiographical memory is the first-person account of a person's life, emotions, and experiences. Children develop richer representations of episodic memory and autobiographical memory with increasing age, and there are debates about how early autobiographical memory emerges. Some studies suggest it emerges as early as four years old, with others suggesting it could be even earlier. This topic centers on whether babies can encode memories successfully but are perhaps not able to store them until they are toddlers[10], but is beyond the scope of this book.

Around 2006 a new type of memory was discovered: **highly superior autobiographical memory** or HSAM, also called hyperthymesia. At first, there were only a few known cases, including the well-known US actress and TV star Marilu Henner. Over time, more cases have emerged, including a child around the age of ten and a more recent case of a 17-year-old teenager in France[11]. She is referred to by her initials, TL, to protect her identity. These children can recall, in very specific and accurate detail, memories from every day of their lives, no matter how mundane. It is so unusual and specific that when TL first described her memories to her friends they accused her of lying. Most people cannot remember what they had for breakfast on a specific day of the week many years ago and cannot tell you what day of the week it was on a random date from the past. However, people with HSAM can do just that. Scientists study them to gain a better understanding of their brain structure and function.

In other aspects of memory, such as doing a digit span task, they do not appear to have exceptional memories. Yet, when a person with HSAM is asked to recall any event or detail from their past, they can do this perfectly. Studying children with HSAM may not only allow the field to benefit from their experiences but also allow the children to move past painful or sad memories from their past. Reliving every personal experience in detail is not always a good thing. The individuals with HSAM differ in how they feel about their unique memory ability, and research continues to explore the ways in which people with HSAM function in their daily lives.

Structure of Memory Systems and Their Interconnections

In Chapter 2 I discuss the basics of the brain and how it is structured, and introduce the case study of Henry Molaison. We learned from his unique case that the hippocampus is critically important in the transfer of information from working memory into long-term memory. One of the things that he and other patients with damage to the hippocampus have shown us is that the hippocampus is involved in declarative memories, or the type of memories that a person can describe or talk about. Mr Molaison was a polite, friendly person and his personality did not change after his surgery, but he was unable to remember meeting new people or details of a conversation after a short period of time had passed. However, he could learn new things when they depended on procedural memories. His implicit, or non-declarative, memory was intact.

Researchers working with Mr Molaison used a task that involves tracing a pattern while looking in the mirror (instead of looking down at the hand doing the tracing). It is a difficult task because the image in the mirror is reversed and it takes time to learn how to do this task effectively. He showed improvement in this task over several days; however, he could not remember working on the task and could not describe it[12]. This example illustrates the distinction between the declarative parts of memory that we call episodic and semantic, and the implicit or non-declarative parts of memory that contribute to things like skills and habits (I describe this as procedural memory earlier in the chapter).

In addition to thinking about how children's ability to remember more items improves with age, researchers have asked questions about the relationship between items in working memory and how they are transferred to long-term memory for future storage. In general, we know that younger children, such as six-year-olds, remember fewer items than older children, such as 12-year-olds. Is children's lower performance in long-term memory tasks the result of limitations in long-term memory alone, or a combination of working memory and long-term memory limitations? Research by Alicia Forsberg and colleagues[13] suggests that the structural factors that control the transfer of information from working memory to long-term memory operate in a similar way in children and adults.

They studied groups of children from 1st to 7th grades and a group of young adults. As you may expect, the young adults and the oldest children remembered more items overall in both a working memory task and a long-term memory recognition task. However, what was most interesting was that the ability to remember information in working memory was related to how many items were retained in the long-term memory task, and this was true for all age groups. This finding suggests that the differences in young children's memory abilities overall are not because they have a limited ability to transfer items from their working memory into their long-term memory. Figure 4.4 illustrates the bi-directional nature of information flowing between working memory and long-term memory. The findings from this study suggest that there is no need to draw different figures to illustrate the flow of information for children as young as six compared to older children or adults. Figure 4.4 shows the movement of information between working memory and long-term memory regardless of whether a child is six or 12 years old.

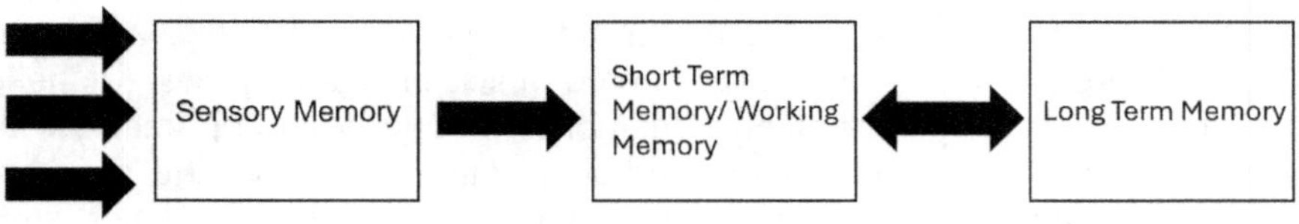

Figure 4.4 The directional relationship between types of information in the memory system. After entering the processing system through sensory memory, new information can move through the short-term memory/working memory system into long-term memory. However, information in long-term memory can influence the way items are processed in short-term memory/working memory as well.

Take-Away Points

- Short-term memory is immediate memory of events in your life, and it lasts about 30 seconds.
- Children's short-term memory capacity increases with age. Sometimes it may seem that children are not listening when in fact the amount of information available may exceed their memory capacity.
- Working memory is a more complex and interactive form of memory than short-term memory.
- In general, people have a smaller working memory capacity than short-term memory. Short-term memory is seven plus or minus two items, while working memory capacity is four plus or minus one.
- Long-term memory is the storehouse of a lifetime of knowledge and experiences. It is subdivided into memories that you can talk about or describe (explicit or declarative memory) and memories that you can put into action but have trouble describing (implicit or procedural memory). Procedural memory is also sometimes called muscle memory.
- Within declarative memory, researchers have found evidence for two subsystems. Episodic memory relates to individual life experiences and semantic memory relates to shared knowledge and facts.

Chapter Summary

Short-term memory and working memory are both very short: about 30 seconds. Long-term memory can be divided into the procedural and declarative systems (the memories of how to do things and the memories you can talk about). The declarative system can be divided into episodic and semantic memory. Episodic memories are details of your own life while semantic memory contains facts that are shared by many people. Evidence for the distinctions of memory have emerged from both experimental studies in laboratories and from patients who have suffered illness or brain injuries. Michelle Miller[14] sums it all up very nicely: "memory isn't one system but many, with separate parts that handle longer- and shorter-term retention and also that deal with distinct kinds of information within these long- and short-term subsystems".

Notes

1 Weinstein, Y. Learning Scientists Blog. https://arc.duke.edu/how-long-is-short-term-memory-shorter-than-you-might-think/
2 Ebbinghaus, H. (1885/1964). *Memory: A contribution to experimental psychology*. Teachers College, Columbia University.

3 Jacobs, J. (1887). Experiments on "prehension". *Mind, 12*, 75–79.
4 Elliott, E. M., Morey, C. C. & AuBuchon, A. et al. (2021). Multilab direct replication of Flavell, Beach, and Chinsky (1966): Spontaneous verbal rehearsal in a memory task as a function of age. *Advances in Methods and Practices in Psychological Science*. http://dx.doi.org.libezp.lib.lsu.edu/10.1177/25152459211018187
5 Cowan, N. (2017). The many faces of working memory and short-term storage. *Psychonomic Bulletin & Review, 24*, 1158–1170. https://doi.org/10.3758/s13423-016-1191-6
6 Case, R., Kurland, D. M., & Goldberg, J. (1982). Operational efficiency and the growth of short-term memory span. *Journal of Experimental Child Psychology, 33*(3), 386–404. https://doi.org/10.1016/0022-0965(82)90054-6
7 Brains On Podcast (August 8, 2023). How much can your brain hold? www.brainson.org/
8 Squire, L. R. & Zola, S. M. (1996). Structure and function of declarative and non-declarative memory systems. *Proceedings of the National Academy of Sciences, 93*(24), 13515–13522. https://doi.org/10.1073/pnas.93.24.13515
9 Rosenbaum, R. S., Köhler, S., Schacter, D. L., Moscovitch, M., Westmacott, R., Black, S. E., Gao, F. & Tulving, E. (2005). The case of K.C.: contributions of a memory-impaired person to memory theory. *Neuropsychologia*. *43*(7),989–1021. https://doi.org/10.1016/j.neuropsychologia.2004.10.007
10 Ramsaran, A. I. & Frankland, P. W. (2025). Babies form fleeting memories. *Science, 387*(6740), 1253–1254. https://doi.org/10.1126/science.adw1923
11 Dolan, E. W. (2025). Teenager with hyperthymesia exhibits extraordinary mental time travel abilities. www.psypost.org/teenager-with-hyperthymesia-exhibits-extraordinary-mental-time-travel-abilities/
12 National Public Radio. Fresh Air. (June 6, 2013). www.npr.org/2013/06/06/187328826/the-patient-who-let-us-peek-inside-a-brain-in-present-tense
13 Forsberg, A., Guitard, D., Adams, E. J., Pattanakul, D. & Cowan, N. (2022). Children's long-term retention is directly constrained by their working memory capacity limitations. *Developmental Science, 25*(2), e13164. https://doi.org/10.1111/desc.13164
14 Miller, M. D. (2024). A teacher's guide to learning student names: Why you should, why it's hard, how you can. University of Oklahoma Press: p. 69.

Chapter 5

What is Attention and What Does It Have to Do with Remembering?

Attention and Encoding New Information

Attention and memory are particularly interesting to me and I have studied them for more than 30 years. What does "attention" means to you? It might be something like "It's how you make yourself focus on the forms you have to fill out for your continuing education workshop", or when your partner says, "Turn off that social media and pay attention to what I'm saying!".

However, while the concept of attention seems very clear, it is one of those topics that becomes more complicated the more you think about it. It gets especially complicated when a researcher studies it in the laboratory. It is very difficult to measure exactly where a person is directing their attention at any given moment. It is something internal and people may not even have control of their attention all the time. Sometimes you can be distracted by something happening around you; this is an example of an external factor recruiting your attentional focus. There are also times when thoughts pop into your head, which is an example of an internal factor leading to an attentional switch. Other examples of internal "switching" factors are thinking about feeling hungry or tired. Studying mind wandering and other off-task behaviors provides some helpful information about attention[1], but the whole notion of attention is much more complex than measuring any one aspect.

In addition to having either an external or internal focus of attention, the ways people apply their attentional resources can differ. Certain tasks require focused attention over time, often called **sustained** attention. On the other hand, someone may rapidly move their attentional focus between different tasks or inputs. In this case, researchers talk about **divided** attention[2]. Bearing both aspects of attention in mind is useful when considering how to best set up an environment to support children's learning and memory.

Sustained Attention

Sustained attention means that attentional focus, or the contents of your current consciousness, is dedicated on one task or event. Sustained attention

DOI: 10.4324/9781003672814-7

can be measured by asking people questions about the material they were reading, or listening to, at a certain time. While there are multiple ways to assess sustained attention, one way that it is measured in children uses a computer task. In one study, children were shown different pictures and were then asked to make judgments about the pictures, such as "Is this a living or a non-living item?"[3] The picture could be a rabbit, which is living, or a box of crayons, which is non-living. The children pressed a button on the keyboard to respond and later were asked in a surprise memory test if they remembered a particular picture. This task requires vigilance or maintaining sustained attention. Children aged seven to ten had more frequent lapses of attention than adults; these attentional lapses also related to memory performance. Judging that an item was "living" was rarer in this task than "non-living", and in the rare trials the children's performance on categorizing was significantly worse than adults. Overall, however, when children were attending to the task, their memory performance was not significantly different than the adults'. This finding indicates that in certain circumstances children's memory performance can be equal to that of adults; yet there are differences in the ways in which children deployed and maintained their attentional focus compared to the adults in this study. It appears that to truly understand why and how children's memories may be different to adults, we must study attention too.

Distraction and Multi-tasking

As mentioned above, another way that attention is studied is by creating situations that lead to divided attention. In everyday life, this can happen if you are trying to read a recipe while simultaneously watching a video on a different topic. Even though it may seem that you can do two things at the same time, research indicates that there are quick shifts between the two different tasks, or rapid switching of attentional resources between two sources. People may feel there is not a cost in trying to do two things simultaneously, but we have learned that people make more mistakes and take longer to complete one of the two tasks than if they were only doing one thing at a time.

Some studies have examined behaviors in terms of how automatically they can be completed compared to how much cognitive effort, or controlled processing, they require. Examining whether a task can be completed with little to no conscious effort helps us to understand the difference between automatic and controlled processing (see Box 5.1). In adults reading in their native language, the amount of cognitive effort can be very low. Adults have spent many years developing reading skills. However, if the text they are reading is complex or difficult, or they are placed in demanding conditions, such as reading in poor lighting in a noisy room, even a familiar task like reading can become difficult. Cognitive psychologists use experimental manipulations in the laboratory to understand this continuum of processing and how tasks can move from being relatively easy, requiring low cognitive effort and being completed quickly, to the opposite side of the continuum that requires complete focus and high levels of cognitive effort. When tasks move to requiring controlled processing like this, it can also mean that they will take longer to complete.

Box 5.1 The continuum of levels of processing from no awareness to highly focused

HIGH LEVEL OF AWARENESS

Controlled Processes

- focused attention, high level of concentration

Automatic Processes

- some awareness, but minimal attention required
- daydreaming, "autopilot"

Unconscious

- due to head injury, anesthesia, and coma

NO AWARENESS

In my research on automatic and controlled processing, I studied what happens when two items are presented to someone at the same time in two different ways. For example, if a colored square is shown on a computer screen, and your job is to name the color, you can answer quickly and easily. However, in my research we also ask people to wear headphones while naming the colors on the screen, and we sometimes present color words over the headphones. Even if you tell someone that they can ignore anything they hear over the headphones, and that they will not be tested on it in any way, we have found that hearing a color word that does not match the color shown on the screen can cause a person to take longer to name the color. Thus, seeing a red color patch on the computer screen while simultaneously hearing "blue" through headphones causes people to slow down their response and to make more errors. This research interested me because it illustrates that we do not always have complete control over our sensory environments. Even telling participants "not to listen" did not help them to avoid this conflict effect.

The color-naming task is based upon a very well-known and often-used paradigm known as the Stroop color-word test. It is named after the person who did his doctoral dissertation on word reading and color naming, John Ridley Stroop, back in 1935[4]. If someone is asked to read the word "green", they can do this quickly and accurately. However, if someone is asked to name the font color of the word "blue", and it is written in green, the conflict between seeing the word blue written in green font leads to slowing down and making more errors[5].

Although there are different theoretical explanations for why this conflict occurs which are beyond the scope of this book, the best-known version focuses on the role of reading. The relatively automatic behavior of reading comes into conflict with the less practiced task of naming the font color of the word. This example illustrates the continuum of automatic and controlled processing and how adults can move back and forth along this continuum. Younger children develop automatic and controlled processes as well, but it takes them longer to, for example, develop the same level of expertise in a task like reading as older children and adults.

To examine if children too young to read would demonstrate a Stroop-like interference effect, researchers developed a child-friendly version of the task[6]. Using well-known objects instead of printed words, the researchers found that children between three-and-a-half to six-and-a-half years of age did demonstrate a Stroop-like interference effect. However, this experiment had to be modified to allow children this young to be tested, as reading is a skill that takes years to develop. This shows how important it is for adults to remember that children who are learning to read need more time and can tire more easily than older children and adults. The amount of attention control and cognitive effort required by younger children is much greater than that required by older people.

Given what was learned about the negative effects of multi-tasking in adults from the Stroop paradigm, researchers have studied children to explore sustained attention and attention-switching abilities with increasing age[7]. One study asked children aged seven to ten to monitor different images of timers on a screen. They used different types of timers, such as a progress bar that filled up as more time was spent on the task. Increasing from two to three timers had a significant impact on the children, especially the youngest. With increasing age, children were better able to monitor three timers.

The researchers included a separate measure of sustained attention, which is an important way to estimate attentional abilities that are separate from the main task. Overall, the conclusions suggested that even children as young as seven can monitor two timers, but the move to three timers was much harder for them. Behavior in this task was related to an individual's ability to sustain attention and to their working memory capacity.

Although the youngest children struggled the most with the multiple timers, they showed evidence of multi-tasking abilities. The improvement of multi-tasking abilities seemed to level off in the eight to nine-year-old children in this study. This finding is consistent with other research on the developmental trajectory of attentional abilities. More work needs to be done in this area to help us to understand the costs of switching attention when asking younger children to monitor multiple sources of information, such as completing time-based tasks in the classroom and/or switching between different tasks. This research also connects to the ideas of automatic and controlled processing, and how this continuum develops during childhood. Asking younger children to do more cognitively taxing tasks causes them to feel more fatigue than older children, which can lead to distracted performance in the classroom.

What does all this research tell us? It seems multi-tasking causes you to take longer to finish what you are doing and make more mistakes while doing your main task. The ability to multi-task is also affected by the type of tasks that are involved. Can a person fold the laundry while watching a show? Yes, they can. But even with this relatively simple task, the person will slow down their folding when a particularly intense scene occurs in their show. We often do two things at once, especially when the two tasks are different in content (listening to music while cooking, for example). Yet when you must concentrate your mental effort on one aspect of the task, the secondary task fades into the background. This example is why drivers may turn down the music in the car if conditions change, such as driving in a complicated intersection or an unfamiliar area. The relatively automatic behavior of driving becomes a controlled process when conditions become more challenging.

Questions about multi-tasking also relate to the concept of an "attention span" and whether there have been recent changes in how long people can direct their attention towards one task. There are different schools of thought about how long someone can sustain attention, and how they perform in the case of divided attention. One aspect is the availability of technology and how it has influenced our attention span. Has our rapid access to a wide range of information changed our ability to sustain attention? I talk about this in more detail in Chapter 8.

Developmental Trajectory of Divided Attention in Children

As discussed in the section on sustained attention, researchers use different methodologies to understand how children's ability to direct their attention to a task, and to shift their attention in response to task demands, can change with age. One team of researchers investigated the age at which children's attentional ability begins to approximate that of adults when remembering information presented in two different locations. They studied children of six and eight years, along with a sample of young adults[8]. The participants were presented with a row of stimuli that were described as a game to help a character find their favorite number. Creating child-friendly instructions helps to improve engagement with the task and makes it more appealing for the children. The adults were given the same task and instructions and were told that it was also designed for use with children. I suspect that the adults did not mind having an engaging explanation for the task, even if it was child oriented.

The researchers then cued certain locations on the screen by changing the color of the items' location before a number appeared. The aim of the task was to type the number that had been shown on the screen. If the location had been previously cued, participants were more accurate in their responses. Sometimes the researchers used cues that were not valid, i.e. they did not predict the location where the number would appear. The researchers used the invalid cues in different locations to investigate how "spread out" the focus of attention could be. The analogy that is often used here is a spotlight on a stage. Is it a single beam of light, focused narrowly on one person on the stage? Or is it a wider beam of light that is broad enough to capture multiple people?

Another question the researchers asked was: if more than one cue was provided, how would the children respond? Would they split their attention and only focus on one cue, or would they try to spread out their attention and focus on both? The difference in results when the cue predicted the location of the number, versus providing an invalid cue, revealed the beneficial role of attention in this task. The results indicated overall that the eight-year-old children were able to perform similarly to adults and benefitted from the valid cues. This benefit was obtained even when two different locations were cued that were not next to each other on the screen. However, the six-year-old children did not show the same benefit when the cues were in two locations.

These findings suggest that the younger children were still developing their ability to deploy their attention across two locations. In essence, the younger children may have been picking one location instead of trying to keep both actively in mind. The older children were successfully deploying their attention across the two locations, like the adults. This study supports the suggestion that children's attentional abilities become more adult-like around eight years of age. It also highlights the ways in which younger children's attentional processes are still changing and developing.

Attention Deficit Hyperactivity Disorder and Memory

The studies described above focused on typically developing children. However, I am often asked about children with a condition such as ADHD and how it may interact with memory functioning. Multiple factors can influence memory and attention, covering other developmental concerns such as learning disabilities or mood disorders; however, those topics are beyond the scope of this book.

While cognitive psychologists often study topics like memory and attention, we do not engage in any type of diagnostic work and cannot provide any formal diagnoses. Parents, teachers, or other family members who have concerns about a child's performance in the classroom could see a licensed psychologist, a pediatrician, or another type of medical specialist. Schools can also refer children for testing and assessment. Child psychologists specialize in the assessment, diagnosis, and treatment of different types of cognitive and behavioral challenges, including learning disabilities and ADHD.

The worldwide prevalence rates of ADHD in children are estimated to be around 7 per cent, with slightly lower rates in adolescents of around 5.5 per cent[9] . In the US, a higher estimate was obtained by researchers who used data from a National Survey of Children's Health, which included both children and adolescents in the estimate[10]. The higher estimate was based upon the criterion of parent report, which is a very useful way to estimate prevalence rates. However, multiple methods are often needed to verify the diagnosis, which may have contributed to the higher estimate obtained in this study. According to the Centers for Disease Control, estimates in the US range from as low as 8 per cent in girls to as high as 15 per cent in boys[11]. This large range of prevalence rates is in part because the ways that girls tend to show inattentive behaviors can be different than boys, and the ways that boys show hyperactivity can be different than girls. Nonetheless, it is very likely that an elementary school classroom will have one or more children with ADHD.

How does the presence of ADHD interact with memory functioning? One way to answer this question is to conduct a meta-analysis, which I discussed in Chapter 3. In a meta-analysis by Ramos and colleagues[12], the research team focused on the relationship of ADHD in children and adolescents and a measure of working memory known as the backward digit span task. Thus, their search of existing published articles focused only on two groups: those with neurotypical children and adolescents as a control group, and children and adolescents with ADHD.

The backward digit span task (Figure 5.1) is a commonly used measure of working memory that can be administered in clinical settings as well as in laboratory research. Children and/or adolescents are presented with a series of numbers in a random order, such as "6, 2, 9, 4" and asked to report them to the examiner in backwards order. The correct answer in this example is "4, 9, 2, 6". This task requires focused and sustained attention, maintaining the items in memory, and the ability to re-order them successfully. Because of its multiple components, this task taps into working memory.

Ramos and colleagues included research studies with children and adolescents who ranged in age from six to 18. It is more typical for children to receive

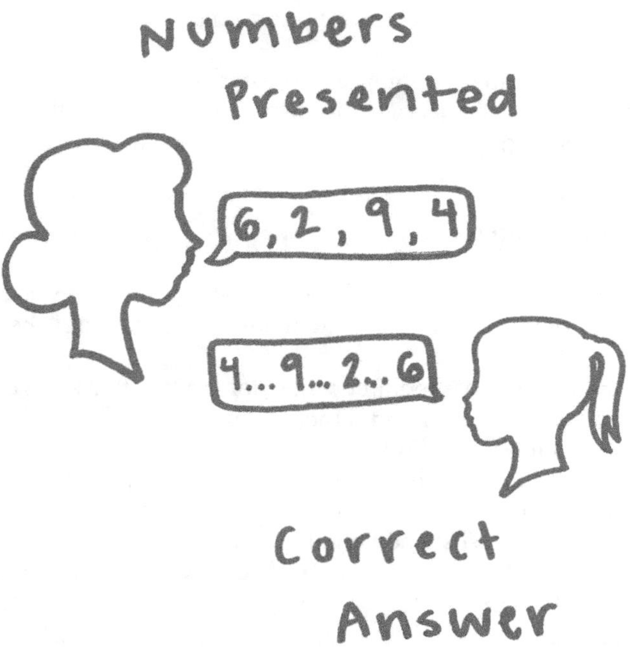

Figure 5.1 Design of the backward digit span task. The participant is given a list of numbers to remember; for the answer to be considered completely correct, the numbers must be reported in backwards order.

a diagnosis of ADHD once they have started formal schooling, thus it is more common to see published studies that do not include children younger than five. The final meta-analysis included 49 published studies from 1990–2016. The combined sample from previous studies included 4956 children/adolescents with ADHD and 3249 control participants. The results indicated a significant decrease in performance on the backward digit span task for individuals with ADHD compared to the control participants. Additionally, the analysis revealed that the difference between the two groups of participants was greater at younger ages and decreased with increasing age. Thus, as children grew older and moved into adolescence, the difference in performance on the digit span backwards task between the two groups became smaller.

These findings, and other published studies, indicate that individuals with ADHD often present with poorer performance on measures of working memory, with implications for both reading and math skills[13]. Researchers have used multiple measures of working memory to assess different aspects of the concept and have begun to work on the idea of interventions that might improve working memory performance in children[14]. However, this research has had limited success in improving performance across a range of tasks and/or behaviors[15].

This topic of cognitive training is discussed in more detail in Chapter 8. Whether or not working memory itself may be changed, there are several strategies and techniques to help children to manage the symptoms of ADHD.

Take-Away Points

- Attention and memory are closely linked so it is often necessary to consider both the attentional demands of a task and the memory demands.
- Sustained attention is required when doing a task that takes controlled processing, or focused and directed cognitive effort. Automatic processing requires less effort.
- Paying attention, as the phrase implies, comes with a cost. Younger children tire more quickly and easily than older children when doing tasks that require sustained and focused attention.
- Children with ADHD often have difficulty with working memory, but there are strategies to support their performance in the classroom.

Chapter Summary

Attention is difficult to define and measure. People can respond to external factors in their environment or to internal factors. Researchers have studied both sustained and divided attention scenarios to understand how much control we exert over our attention and memory in any given task. Sustained attention requires conscious effort and focus and can lead to mental and physical fatigue. Divided attention can also lead to mental and physical fatigue. Children as young as six can multi-task, or rapidly switch between tasks, and this ability improves with age. Being aware of challenges to attention and working memory can help teachers, parents, and caregivers guide children to achieve optimum performance in the classroom.

Notes

1 Cherry, J., McCormack, T. & Graham, A. J. (2024). Listen up, kids! How mind wandering affects immediate and delayed memory in children. *Memory & Cognition, 52*, 909–925.
https://doi.org/10.3758/s13421-023-01509-0
2 Kiesel, A., Johannsen, L., Koch, I., & Müller, H. (Eds). (2022). *Handbook of human multitasking*. Springer Nature.

3 Decker, A. L., Duncan, K. & Finn, A. S. (2023). Fluctuations in sustained attention explain moment-to-moment shifts in children's memory formation. *Psychological Science, 34*(12), 1377–1389. https://doi.org/10.1177/09567976231206767.
4 Stroop, J. R. (1935). Studies of interference in serial verbal reactions. *Journal of Experimental Psychology, 18*(6), 643–662. https://doi.org/10.1037/h0054651
5 Medina, V. A., Lutfi-Proctor, D. A. & Elliott, E. M. (2022). The role of joint influence on the cross-modal Stroop effect: Investigating time course and asymmetry. *Auditory Perception & Cognition.* https://doi.org/10.1080/25742442.2022.2034394
6 Prevor, M. B. & Diamond, A. (2005). Color–object interference in young children: A Stroop effect in children 3½–6½ years old. *Cognitive Development, 20*(2), 256–278. https://doi.org/10.1016/j.cogdev.2005.04.001
7 Frick, A., Chavaillaz, A., Mäntylä, T. & Kubik, V. (2022). Development of multitasking abilities in middle childhood. *Learning and Instruction, 77,* 101540. https://doi.org/10.1016/j.learninstruc.2021.101540
8 Blankenship, T. L., Strong, R. & Kibbe, M. M. (2026). The ability to divide spatial attention across non-contiguous locations develops in middle childhood. *Attention, Perception, & Psychophysics, 88,* 9. https://doi.org/10.3758/s13414-025-03182-8
9 Salari, N., Ghasemi, H., Abdoli, N. et al. (2023). The global prevalence of ADHD in children and adolescents: A systematic review and meta-analysis. *Italian Journal of Pediatrics, 49*, 48. https://doi.org/10.1186/s13052-023-01456-1
10 Zgodic, A., McLain, A. C., Eberth, J. M., Federico, A., Bradshaw, J. & Flory, K. (2023). County-level prevalence estimates of ADHD in children in the United States. *Annals of Epidemiology, 79,* 56–64. https://doi.org/10.1016/j.annepidem.2023.01.006
11 Centers for Disease Control and Prevention (CDC) . Data on ADHD in children. www.cdc.gov/adhd/data/index.html
12 Ramos, A. A., Hamdan, A. C. & Machado, L. (2020). A meta-analysis of verbal working memory in children and adolescents with ADHD. *The Clinical Neuropsychologist, 34*(5), 873–898. https:/doi.org/10.1080/13854046.2019.1604998
13 Gaye, F., Groves, N. B., Chan, E. S. M., Cole, A. M., Jaisle, E. M., Soto, E. F. & Kofler, M. J. (2023). Working memory and math skills in children with and without ADHD. *Neuropsychology, 38*(1), 1–16. https://doi.org/10.1037/neu0000920.
14 Spencer-Smith, M., Quach, J., Mensah, F., Roberts, G., Gathercole, S., Wake, M. & Anderson, P. J. (2020). The effectiveness of working memory training for children with low working memory. *Pediatrics, 146*(6), e20194028. https://doi.org/10.1542/peds.2019-4028
15 Gobet, F. & Sala, G. (2023). Cognitive training: A field in search of a phenomenon. *Perspectives on Psychological Science, 18*(1), 125–141. https://doi.org/10.1177/17456916221091830

Chapter 6

Forgetting: Is It Always a Bad Thing?

We receive large amounts of information constantly from the senses, such as sights, sounds, and smells. These are ongoing external events. We also have internal events such as our bodily state (e.g., are we hungry or thirsty?) and our emotional state (e.g., are we angry or frustrated?). As discussed in Chapter 5, if a person does not focus on or attend to information, it is very difficult to remember it later. Yet forgetting something you need to remember is a negative experience. How do we understand when forgetting is a good thing, and the times when it is not?

Researchers have studied forgetting in working memory by examining the effect of having repetitions of items or stimuli across the parts of a memory task. If a participant is asked to remember a set of items in one trial and then is given some of the same stimuli again but in a different location or in a different order, the previous presentation of the stimuli can make it more difficult to remember the later stimuli[1]. We call this phenomenon "**proactive interference**", sometimes abbreviated as PI.

In terms of proactive interference in working memory, I previously discussed the concept of working memory and how it can be measured using a complex span task. In complex span tasks, participants are asked to learn a series of items for a later memory test, and in between the presentation of each item, they are asked to do a different task such as solving a math problem. At the end of a sequence of memory items and math problems, the goal is to remember the memory items in the order they were presented.

One way to reduce the build up of proactive interference across a sequence of trials is to change the type of memory item. If the initial memory items were letters, changing them to numbers partway through the experiment can help memory performance because switching to a different type of item releases the build-up of any proactive interference during the experiment[2].

In this case, before switching the memory items from numbers to letters, the prior information reaches forward and can make it harder to remember which letter was part of the most current set. A series of trials with letters coming one after the other can make it more difficult to remember which letters occurred in each trial. Switching to numbers as the to-be-remembered items

DOI: 10.4324/9781003672814-8

thus "frees up" this interference, which is why we call it "release from PI". You may have experienced proactive interference when looking for your parked car. If you typically drive to the same parking lot and have often parked there, it can be difficult to remember exactly where you parked your car on a particular trip. You may even find yourself walking to a spot where you parked in the past, only to realize your car is not there. This difficulty in finding your car can be made worse if you were also distracted when you were parking. Did you get a call or did someone start talking to you while you were getting out of the car? A distracted focus of attention can make it harder to remember something later. When you add the fact that there is also proactive interference from previous trips to this parking lot, it is clear how the factors of interference and divided attention can make it hard to find your car sometimes.

Proactive Interference in Children

Proactive interference has been studied extensively in adults as a mechanism of forgetting, but studies on proactive interference in children are much more limited. One important study was conducted on children as young as two-and-a-half[3], and used pictures of items on a screen in a computer analog of a card-matching memory game. Colored squares were shown on a screen, and the pictures behind the squares were revealed when the child tapped on the location. This task design is similar to the card game that requires players to look for matching cards by remembering the location of the cards, but one can only see the picture on the card when it is flipped over. The players have to learn and remember the identity of the card based upon the location, because they can no longer see the item once the card is flipped back over. The researchers found reliable effects of the repeated presentation of items across the trials of the study, which was interpreted as clear evidence of proactive interference. When the children were shown the same images multiple times across the trials, performance declined more than when repeated pictures were not used. In terms of the matching card game analogy, this manipulation would be similar to shuffling the deck, starting a new game, and using the same few pictures over and over. It becomes more difficult to differentiate between which time a certain picture appeared in a certain location when the images are repeated.

The researchers completed three experiments and used high-quality methodology to replicate their own findings. Overall, the researchers found that even toddlers perform better on this item-location memory task when the items were not repeated across trials, showing evidence for the mechanism of proactive interference as a means of forgetting. The authors also discussed the implications of these findings for children in the classroom. When teaching similar concepts to children, it can be helpful to break them up and provide different types of material across learning sessions, as opposed to presenting all of one concept at a time, followed by the whole of a second concept at a time. This method is often referred to as interleaving, as opposed to a blocked presentation.

Proactive interference is one way that forgetting can occur in our daily lives. Yet, for most people the small details of daily life do not need to be remembered. Is it really important to remember what you had for breakfast on a certain day five years ago? Forgetting is a healthy way for our memory systems to focus on the most critical elements and clean out the small details that we do not need.

Another aspect of forgetting is to consider whether the information was truly learned or attended to in the first place. As discussed in Chapter 2, cognitive psychologists call the process of taking in new information "encoding". In this process people focus their attention on something and intentionally try to remember it. However, we often encounter small details that we do not need to try to save for later. The sheer volume of information around us in our daily lives means that it is impossible to notice and remember everything. Thus, sometimes we do not look very closely, especially if the details are not relevant to the task that we are currently completing. One example that is often used in cognitive psychology textbooks to illustrate this idea of "encoding failure" is to show several pictures of a penny. Before the US stopped using pennies, how often did you look closely at them? You could recognize one and knew how to use them, but did you ever attend to the words written on the coin, or the direction in which President Lincoln's head was facing? If asked to pick out the exact details of a penny when presented with other "lures" that looked very close to the original but were not correct, many people were unable to select the correct penny. This example suggests that sometimes we may think we have "forgotten" something, but we never really encoded it in the first place.

Remembering to Do a Future Task

Another aspect of forgetting is a type of memory known as **prospective** memory. Have you told yourself you would stop on the way home from work to pick up a prescription, only to realize you had driven all the way home without it? This type of forgetting is frustrating and is commonly experienced. It involves remembering to do an action in the future[4], such as a child remembering to take their track uniform to school on certain days. Being successful in a task like this involves creating an intention to do something in the future and then carrying out a plan to complete the intention. The ability to do a future task is linked to something else I will discuss: metacognition, or knowing about cognition. Metamemory is focused on knowledge of your own memory performance, such as knowing that you will forget something if you do not leave yourself a sticky note or other type of reminder. I discuss this in more detail Chapter 7, as it is an important aspect of childhood cognitive development.

Children's metamemory and prospective memory skills develop through childhood and into adolescence[5]. Researchers have examined different strategies to help children to become more aware of their own knowledge of memory and to support the successful formation of intentions. Prospective memory performance can be improved through interventions[6] such as asking a child to imagine completing a task before actually doing it. It is important to understand these interventions so that we can help children to act independently and build their own habits and skills around successful memory strategies. One of the findings that has emerged from the literature is that prospective memory studied in a laboratory setting does not always compare exactly with prospective memory behaviors in real life[7].

To address this concern in a group of children seven to nine years old, researchers devised a real-world task with practical implications. The children were given the real-world task of taking a letter home from school, giving it to their parents, and bringing it back to school the next day. The researchers also used a questionnaire that was completed by parents and caregivers to give information on the children's prospective memory (such as completing an item in the future) and retrospective memory (such as remembering going on a trip in the past).

The children were recruited to participate in this study from 12 2nd and 3rd-grade classes across six different schools. They were divided into four groups, a control and three experimental. In the control group, the teachers were asked to give the children the letter at the beginning of the school day and ask them to bring it back the next day. They were not given any additional information. There were three experimental groups, referred to as prediction, episodic future thinking, and combined. In the "prediction" group, the children were asked to predict how likely they were to complete this task. In the "episodic future thinking" group, the children were asked to do an imagery exercise in which they imagined themselves in detail completing the task. The teachers included details such as asking them to imagine going into their schoolbags to take out the letter at home and give it to their parents. Using episodic future thinking has been shown to be effective in other laboratory-based research on prospective memory. The last group was a combination of the prediction group and the episodic future thinking group.

The children were scored on whether they remembered to bring the letter back to school the next day. Overall, the findings suggested that the three experimental groups had higher rates of letters returned than the control group. Interestingly, the researchers originally predicted that the "prediction + episodic future thinking" group would have the highest rates of return. Statistically speaking, that did not happen. The prediction group, which used a short and simple manipulation of asking children to answer two questions about how likely they were to remember this task, did the best overall. These results show again how the outcomes from real-life prospective memory tasks and laboratory-based prospective memory tasks can differ. It is also encouraging to hear that sometimes the short and simple manipulation is successful. Teachers are very busy in the classroom and likely have developed numerous strategies to help children to remember tasks such as bringing back a letter the next day. Engaging children in two questions to help them predict how likely they are to complete a task seems an easy way to increase prospective memory in children and reduce forgetting.

So far, I have discussed proactive interference as a form of forgetting, as well as encoding failures that lead to the perception of forgetting. I also discussed how creating a future intention to complete a task is more likely to make a child remember to complete an action in the future. These are just some of the ways that forgetting can occur, but it is not an exhaustive account.

As a consistent theme of this book, attention and memory work together to produce successful remembering and can also be implicated when we forget. If forgetting can be explained by understanding how memory and attention work, why does forgetting seem so troublesome? We have many more memory successes than failures daily, yet we often do not notice them. The salience, or how much something stands out to you, is very different for forgetting something important. It can be a hassle to temporarily lose your car keys, especially when in a rush to get somewhere on time. But it may also feel much worse for a child to complete their homework and forget to turn it in, depending on the consequences. The way forgetting can impact our lives may be why we remember the stressful moments when we forgot something, and do not focus on the many times we remembered where we left our car keys. Children experience these moments as well, and it is part of their learning about both successful remembering and annoying moments of forgetting.

Structuring children's environments can give them memory supports to minimize forgetting. Adults and older children learn to leave important items in the same place, such as always leaving your backpack by the door so you remember to grab it on the way out. However, younger children may not even realize the need to use memory cues because they have a different level of metacognition, or knowledge about their own cognition. I discuss this in more detail in Chapter 7 and give some suggestions for how to increase metacognitive behaviors in children. I also revisit this topic in Chapter 9 when I discuss global strategies for improving memory and attention.

Take-Away Points

- Forgetting can occur for different reasons, and different mechanisms of forgetting have been studied in children and adults.
- Forgetting is common and something many people find frustrating.
- One type of "forgetting" happens if a person does not encode the information in the first place; then there is nothing in memory to retrieve.

- Even toddlers can be affected by a type of forgetting known as proactive interference. One way to overcome proactive interference is to mix up the types of information to be remembered so that they stand out from each other. Similarity among items can cause interference.
- Using strategies for prospective memory, or remembering to complete an action in the future, can increase children's performance of future tasks and minimize forgetting.
- Becoming aware of the need to take steps to remember things is a form of metacognition, or knowing about knowing, and children improve in these skills with age.

Chapter Summary

Forgetting can take different forms and has been studied in the laboratory and in the real world. Proactive interference is a form of forgetting that can occur when information from the past reaches forward and interferes with current remembering. Similarly, sometimes we think we have forgotten something, but we really did not learn it in the first place. Maybe our attention was divided at the time of encoding, or it was not important. We do not need to remember everything about the numerous interactions we have every day. Our attention and memory systems work together to help us select what we believe is the most relevant in the moment. Children can be given strategies to remember to complete tasks in the future, and these strategies can minimize forgetting.

Notes

1 Redick, T. S., Wiemers, E. A. & Engle, R. W. (2020) The role of proactive interference in working memory training and transfer. *Psychological Research 84,* 1635–1654.
https://doi.org/10.1007/s00426-019-01172-8

2 Bunting, M. (2006). Proactive interference and item similarity in working memory. *Journal of Experimental Psychology: Learning, Memory, and Cognition, 32*(2), 183–196.
https://doi.org/10.1037/0278-7393.32.2.183.

3 Hamilton, M., Roper, T., Blaser, E. & Kaldy, Z. (2024). Can't get it out of my head: Proactive interference in the visual working memory of 3-to 8-year-old children. *Developmental Psychology, 60*(3), 582–594. https://doi.org/10.1037/dev0001686

4 Shelton, J. T. & Scullin, M. K. (2017). The dynamic interplay between bottom-up and top-down processes supporting prospective memory. *Current Directions in Psychological Science, 26*(4), 352–358. https://doi.org/10.1177/0963721417700504

5 Cottini, M., Basso, D., Pieri, A. & Palladino, P. (2021). Metacognitive monitoring and control in children's prospective memory. *Journal of Cognition and Development, 22*(4), 619–639. https://doi.org/10.1080/15248372.2021.1916500

6 Cottini, M., Palladino, P. & Basso, D. (2024). From the lab to the classroom: Improving children's prospective memory in a natural setting. *British Journal of Educational Psychology, 94*, 809–823. https://doi.org/10.1111/bjep.12682
7 Rummel, J., Snijder, J.-P. & Kvavilashvili, L. (2023). Prospective memories in the wild: Predicting memory for intentions in natural environments. *Memory & Cognition, 51*(5), 1061–1075. https://doi.org/10.3758/s13421-022-01379-y

Chapter 7

What is Metamemory and How Does It Change in Childhood?

One of the many things I love about working with children is their candor. They do not always feel the need to say things in "as nice a way as possible" and they can be very direct. They can also be very generous with their affection. As they get older they lose some of this uninhibited behavior, in part due to development of the frontal lobes but also as the result of learning from numerous social situations and attending formal schooling. Another big reason for this change is their awareness of their own cognition and their own memory ability. Researchers use two terms for this ability: **metacognition** is the broader term that refers to thinking about thinking, whereas **metamemory** is focused on memory processes. For example, if I ask a five-year-old child to help me remember a grocery list, they are likely to willingly agree to help. Children like to help and they like to be included. They are also likely to overestimate their abilities. If I ask this child to help me to remember a five- or six-item list of groceries, they will confidently agree. However, when it is time to tell me the items, they are often unable to remember the entire list. In fact, they may only remember two or three items.

While this outcome may be surprising to adults in this scenario, the children do not seem fazed by this discrepancy and some may not even notice. Thus, there is a disconnect between their knowledge of their memory ability, their confidence, and their willingness to be helpful. This example illustrates why gaining a better understanding of metacognition and metamemory development is critical for helping children to improve their own memory ability.

Metacognition has been a topic of childhood development for a very long time, with some of the most widely recognized research in this area conducted by Flavell[1] in the 1970s. Thinking about thinking turns out to be a critically important skill that is related to how well children can regulate their learning and apply strategies to improve their learning and performance, especially in the classroom. These developments are coupled with increases in memory capacity, attentional control abilities, and emotional development. Thus, several critically important changes happen during childhood development that can explain these improvements in performance.

DOI: 10.4324/9781003672814-9

In Chapter 4 on short-term, working, and long-term memory, I describe research that my colleagues and I conducted in a large, multiple-lab study. We investigated the development of short-term memory span, which is a measure of the ability to repeat a series of items back in the order they were presented. We included an immediate recall condition, and a condition with a 15-second delay between presentation of the items and the recall period. We found that, from five to six to seven and then 10 years of age, children were able to remember more items in order as they matured. We also assessed the degree to which children spontaneously used verbal skills, such as repeating the memory items back to themselves, to improve their performance. This verbal behavior is one example of a strategy, and if children are using these behaviors to improve their memory performance, it suggests a relationship between strategy use and metamemory. In short, the children must realize that they might forget the items and try to find a solution.

The original study included a total of 977 children from 17 different countries. The main findings on age-related improvements in memory span are described in more detail in Chapter 4. We also investigated how likely the children were to engage in strategic behaviors to support their recall. We used the methods of open science, which means in part that we made the experimental materials, protocol, de-identified data, and analyses publicly available on a website through the Open Science Framework[2]. We then went back into the data set, led by Candice Morey[3], and asked more specific questions about the relationship between memory span performance and strategy use. In this case we needed to observe children's direct behaviors, which meant relying on research labs that video-recorded the sessions as opposed to having experimenters in the room making observations in real time. Not every lab recorded the sessions but many did.

We analyzed the recall data and strategic behaviors of a subset of 522 children. One of the findings was that over half of the children did not use any type of strategy that involved repeating the items back to themselves during the 15-second delay between seeing the pictures and having to recall them in order. There were 249 children that named the pictures during the presentation of the stimuli and used a type of repetition behavior during the delay before recall. These two groups were examined to determine if the number of items they could remember in order would differ. It turned out that there was a clear relationship: children who rehearsed remembered more items than children who did not. However, the times when they were more likely to rehearse were affected by the number of items in a particular list. The task started by showing children two pictures, in order, that needed to be remembered. Each child saw two trials of two pictures, which then increased to three, then four, and finally five pictures. What we learned from this study was that the children were most likely to try to remember the items by using a spoken strategy when the list length was within a comfortable zone. We called this a "Goldilocks effect". When a young child was given a longer list, such as four or five items, they did not engage in rehearsal behaviors. However, more rehearsal behaviors were likely when the lists were within their ability level. In the oldest children, we also observed that when the list was too easy, such as only two items, they did not use rehearsal strategies. The list length had to be "just right" for their age for the children to use a strategy such as trying to rehearse the items that needed to be remembered.

After the task was finished, we asked the children in our study about the ways in which they tried to complete it. We recorded their responses and then went back to the answers in the recall task to compare their awareness of using strategies with how many items they could remember in order. What we observed was consistent with the casual conversations people may have had with children in other settings. The youngest children, the five-year-olds, found it difficult to tell us if they had used any strategies. Also, their performance was not always consistent across the task. Just because a child decided to use a memory strategy in one part of the task did not mean that they would use that same strategy every time. For example, older children were more likely to use a cumulative strategy, such as repeating the first item in a list after they saw it and then adding that rehearsal to the second item and so forth. If they were shown three pictures (an owl, an apple, and a pencil), a cumulative strategy might sound like this: "owl, owl, owl: owl, apple, owl, apple, owl, apple: pencil, owl, apple, pencil". This type of strategy is not only more difficult, but it takes more time to repeat the picture names between the presentation of the pictures. The younger children were more likely to use a strategy of reporting only the item from each list once, like "owl, owl, owl: apple, apple, apple," as opposed to using a cumulative strategy.

Overall, we found that with increasing age, children became better able to effectively use strategies in this task when the lists were "just right" in length. We believe that these results are due to both maturation and increasing metacognitive awareness; however, we did not include any direct measures of metacognition such as a self-report survey in our study. We made these conclusions based upon the recall data and the connections between the recall data and the strategic behaviors of rehearsal.

Studying Teacher Language to Improve Metacognition in Children

Beyond having additional direct measures of metacognition, there are two other aspects of this study that I want to highlight as clear directions for future research. One is that it was conducted in a laboratory setting, and second, the individual children may have differed in more ways than just their chronological age. When considering the application of metacognition and metamemory in real-life settings, it is important to examine tasks and actions that extend beyond the controlled environment of a laboratory. It is also important to think about the individual children and differences in their backgrounds and abilities, so that any interventions we might introduce can be as effective as possible.

One group of researchers addressed both points in a study on metamemory and the development of memory strategies in children[4]. They wanted to learn more about how teachers talk about memory, strategy use, and metacognition in the classroom. They also wondered about the children themselves and how they tried to adjust their learning in response to different situations. The researchers measured self-regulated learning, which includes behaviors like setting goals and then going back to the goals to determine if they are being met.

This study was conducted with children in the 1st grade who were about six-and-a-half years old when the study started. One of the strengths of this study was that it was longitudinal, which means that the same children were followed over time and tested more than once. Drawing strong conclusions about developmental changes in children is more difficult if the same children are not followed over time, because it can introduce other variables that the researchers cannot account for in their design. This metacognition and teacher language study measured the same children at three points in the 1st grade, and then three more points in the 2nd grade.

Another strength of the study is that the number of participants was not too small, which is sometimes a criticism of research studies. There were 107 children when the study started. Between the 1st and 2nd grades there were some natural changes to the number of children due to factors such as moving or changing schools. There were 91 children in the second year of the study. This study represents a large amount of work, and longitudinal work can be difficult.

The research team worked with teachers across 14 classrooms in four different schools, and the testing and observations started in the fall semester of the 1st-grade year. Measures of both the children's and the teacher's behaviors were recorded. Having both measures allowed the researchers to examine combinations of teacher characteristics, such as how frequently the teachers used language in the classroom that encouraged children to use strategies. An example of teacher metacognitive language given in the study is: "How did you solve that problem? How did you know that you should add?" Children were also rated on how individuals compared with others in terms of how well they used self-regulated learning skills such as the "ability to set goals, organize materials, prepare a place to study ...". The results also took into account short-term memory and working memory differences that may have existed in the children before the study started by having the children complete forward and backward digit span tasks.

Based upon the combinations of teacher and student characteristics, four groups were created: high levels of teacher language that encouraged strategies and metacognition compared to lower levels of teacher language, along with high levels of child self-regulated learning relative to lower levels of self-regulated learning. The combinations were (1) high teacher metacognitive language, high self-regulated child learning (HH); (2) low teacher language, high self-regulated learning (LH); (3) high teacher language, low self-regulated learning (HL); and (4) low teacher language, low self-regulated learning (LL). The children were asked to complete a task that included sorting and understanding different groups of items three times in the 1st grade and then three times in the 2nd grade. This type of task taps into semantic memory, which I discuss in Chapter 4. It is memory of facts and learned information, as opposed to episodic memory, which is personal and related to moments from person's life.

The data indicated that the group with lower levels of metacognitive teacher language and self-regulated learning (LL) had more difficulty with the sorting and categorization task. Higher levels of teacher metacognitive language and higher levels of self-regulated learning (HH), not surprisingly, led to improved performance over time. However, the children with higher levels of metacognitive teacher language who also had lower levels of self-regulated learning (HL) also performed better over time and were not very different from the HH group. Thus, both teacher and student characteristics are very important in how children learn and use metacognition. The findings have important implications for interventions in the classroom, such as encouraging the use of metacognitive language. The group that benefitted the most from the metacognitive teacher language was the group with lower levels of self-regulated learning (HL). These benefits of the 1st-grade metacognitive teacher language carried over into the 2nd grade, when the students had new teachers. Creating greater awareness of children's need to remember, as well as providing strategies to remember, can help children, especially those with lower levels of self-regulated learning in early elementary school.

Direct Instruction in Metacognitive Awareness

Researchers in Romania who wanted to understand the metacognitive behaviors of schoolchildren developed an intervention to determine if metacognition could be increased over time[5]. They focused on two groups of children, five and nine years of age, considered to be at two critically different levels of metacognitive awareness. The five-year-olds were just beginning to understand that they had to be metacognitively aware and could benefit from strategy instructions, whereas the nine-year-olds were more cognitively mature and had more experience in school settings. The researchers adapted a measure that had previously been used in adult populations to make it appropriate for children as young as five. They conducted a ten-week intervention that included embedding the instruction of metacognitive knowledge into activities designed to increase metacognitive knowledge over time (Study

3). A total of 218 children participated in the experimental group and 60 children were in the control group. The activities were carried out in typical classrooms, giving this work the important benefit of having real-world relevance.

The children were asked to engage in metacognitive activities, such as doing a "starter" task at the beginning of the day that was designed to raise their awareness of their metacognitive abilities. Another example of a metacognitive activity was asking the children to identify true and false statements related to their metacognitive awareness. A third activity was for the children to write a letter to their future selves or create a drawing of ways to be successful in future academic tasks. Metacognitive activities were done in the classroom for the first four days of the week, and interviews with the children were conducted on Fridays. In one item on the metacognitive knowledge questionnaire, for example, children were asked to respond to: "After I finish, I can tell if I learned enough."

One of the strengths of this study is that it was conducted in a classroom setting and used a longitudinal design in which the same children were tested over ten weeks. The outcome measure was a questionnaire on the children's knowledge and awareness of their own metacognitive skills. This type of study design tests whether implementing age-appropriate games and activities in the classroom increases children's knowledge of metacognitive skills, which is important. However, it did not include other outcome measures such as academic achievement, so it is difficult to know if increasing knowledge and awareness of metacognition in the children will transfer to other tasks. The findings indicate that the experimental group showed significant gains in their scores on the metacognitive questionnaire. As other research has shown, it also suggested, via interviews and qualitative analysis, that the children who started out with lower metacognitive awareness gained the most. Interestingly, the findings were the same for the five- and nine-year olds, suggesting that both age groups were able to learn about their own metacognition.

Providing directed training and guidance to help children to increase their metacognitive behaviors is one avenue that shows promise. Additionally, researchers have investigated the underlying relationship between metacognitive behaviors and other aspects of cognitive control, such as using laboratory-based tasks to obtain fine-grained measurements of behavior. These tasks typically measure reaction times when responding to stimuli presented on a computer screen as well as accuracy, which is a bit different than a real-world task like learning in the classroom. In an experimental study that investigated the direct training of metacognitive executive functioning[6], researchers worked with 134 children approximately eight years of age. Executive functioning is a broad term that includes concepts like working memory and inhibition of responses, and many researchers believe it is closely linked to the underlying aspects of metacognition.

This study involved three groups: an active control group, a group that was trained in executive functioning alone and a group that was trained in executive functioning plus metacognition. The children completed a battery of tasks to assess baseline differences in cognitive functioning, and then completed 16 training sessions and activities and a post-test.

Overall, the training sessions led to positive gains in working memory performance, relative to the control group. However, the training did not lead to changes in academic performance over the two months of the study. It may be possible to observe improvements over a longer period, but the study did not include later follow-up testing. This type of work is very demanding and requires great effort on the part of the researchers and the participants, yet it is important to help us understand what types of intervention can increase children's performance. By assessing these types of laboratory-based tasks in addition to training metacognitive skills, we can gain a better understanding of the underlying mechanisms and mental processes that support academic performance.

Children's Reasoning about Artificial Intelligence

As AI tools are becoming more widely used, it is important to ask questions about the ways in which children understand AI. Children will not only be asked to develop their own metacognition but will also need to assess the accuracy of interactions with other people and AI tools. From my experience teaching college students, it is clear to me that sometimes very conscientious and intelligent students can be fooled by AI tools. The tools are designed to present their outputs with authority and a tone that makes the user feel flattered by the interaction. This is meant to continue the engagement by making the user feel "smart" or that they are "asking good questions", even if the AI tool is completely wrong about the content. The deliberate tone is called sycophantic. If college students can be lulled into believing the AI tool is correct when it really is not, then what will happen with younger children? They are more likely to grow up using these tools regularly. Thus, the concern about reasoning with AI and identifying errors in the output applies to younger children as well. Learning to identify if the person or AI tool that you are interacting with is giving correct information or not is an element of metacognition and regulation and is a new challenge for the youngest generation.

A team of researchers in Seattle, Washington designed a study to improve our understanding of children's reasoning using AI tools[7]. The researchers used a set of puzzles known as the Abstraction Reasoning Corpus and adapted them to an AI context. To increase the participation and motivation of the children, the resulting AI puzzlers were designed as a game. Children were first asked to solve a puzzle on their own. Then they were given opportunities to interact with a Gen AI tool (in this case it was Chat GPT 4.0). By then comparing how they solved the puzzle by themselves to how they solved it using a Gen AI solution, the children were given the opportunity to evaluate the outcome of the Gen AI tool and gain insight into the errors that were made along the way.

The first step was to engage a large group of children in the puzzles. They presented the AI puzzles to 106 children in grades 3–8 (which is roughly eight to 13 years of age). Overall, the children rated the puzzles as not very difficult. On a scale of 1–5, with 1 indicating the lowest level of difficulty and 5 indicating the highest, the average rating of difficulty was 2.38. This first step was important to gain a sense of the difficulty level of the puzzles before engaging in more research.

Then the researchers engaged 21 children in two sessions during a summer camp program. The children who participated ranged from six to 11 years. During the two sessions, the children worked in small groups with adult research facilitators. They were asked to interact with the AI puzzlers and to evaluate the ways in which the Gen AI tool solved the puzzles. This type of activity is helpful in developing metacognition in children and increases our understanding of how children evaluate errors made by AI tools. The adult facilitators asked the children questions such as: "Do you think Gen AI can solve these puzzles quickly or slowly? Why?" The questions were designed to help the children start their own process of evaluating the Gen AI tool.

The children then interacted with the puzzles and the Gen AI tool. An emerging theme was that children were very surprised by how poorly the Gen AI tool performed. They indicated that they thought the puzzles were easy, yet the Gen AI tool seemed to have difficulty coming to the correct conclusion. The children clearly saw and understood the pattern and the steps that were needed to solve the problem. They also clearly saw that the Gen AI tool did not theorize about the patterns in the same way as they did. The children also showed satisfaction when solving a difficult puzzle; the game aspect of the puzzles incentivized them. This brings up another important dimension that separates us from AI tools, namely, satisfaction and a sense of pride in a job well done. Finally, the children were shown how the Gen AI tool worked "under the hood" to increase their understanding of the model itself and how it generated answers to the puzzles. The children gave the Gen AI tool hints on how to solve the puzzles and could then evaluate the output and determine if additional hints were needed. In this way, the children were helping to train the AI tool to perform the task at a higher level. Overall, seeing the reasoning process of the Gen AI tool in this interactive and engaging way increases AI literacy in children and helps them spot errors that these tools can make in the future.

Research like this is important to increase our understanding of how children reason with AI tools. It is also important to assess the way that adults reason and interact with AI tools to facilitate everyone's ability to spot errors, mistakes, and outright hallucinations made by these tools. In the future it will be important to have continuing and open conversations with children about AI tool use. Building their critical thinking skills helps children evaluate the output of AI tools. Many children already have experience using different types of AI tools, such as voice-activated assistance systems like Alexa™,

Siri™ and Hey Google™. As technology continues to advance, it is important that we know what children think these tools are capable of, and that they recognize when the tools are wrong.

In addition to further research on AI tools in general, more research on the development of metacognition is needed to evaluate the impact of these rapid technological advances on children's understanding of thinking and reasoning. As discussed, there are sometimes differences in the way that behaviors can be explained in a controlled environment like a laboratory and in a real-world setting. This distinction is important in many aspects of children's lives, particularly in prospective memory behaviors like remembering to do a task in the future. The timescale of prospective memory behaviors is often much longer in the real world than in the laboratory, because classroom tasks must sometimes be completed the next day or even the next week. In a similar way, children's memory, attention, and metacognitive skills emerge over time and are tested in different contexts. We need a combination of both laboratory-based and real-world studies to find the best ways to support children and their learning. I return to the concept of cognitive and working memory training in Chapter 8 to discuss when it is likely to be successful and what realistic expectations should be kept in mind when thinking about "brain training" in general.

Take-Away Points

- Metamemory, or a child's awareness of their own memory abilities, is a skill that develops with age. It has been studied by examining the use of strategies in laboratory-based memory tasks.
- Children as young as five show evidence of metamemory ability. However, individual differences exist in how frequently and effectively children can apply such strategies to help with their memory and cognition.
- Teaching children to think about their own thinking, such as modeling behaviors in the classroom and using metacognitive language, may help them to improve their metacognition.
- Talking to children about AI tools and how to reason about the output of AI interactions is a new area of research and can teach children how the tools work and how to spot errors that the AI tools make.

Chapter Summary

Metacognition is the way in which people think about their own thinking. A subset of this term is memory processes, or metamemory. Children's metacognitive abilities develop rapidly, starting around age five. Part of this developmental change is driven by improvements in memory abilities, and part by formal schooling and completing tasks such as tests. Researchers have studied the development of metacognition in both real-world and laboratory-based settings. It is important for us to gain a better understanding of both types of settings so that effective strategies and implementations can be put into action. An area that needs future research is teachers' use of metacognitive language in the classroom to promote children's development of successful strategies, and whether those strategies lead to improvements in cognitive functioning. Teaching children how AI systems can be trained can facilitate their understanding and identification of incorrect reasoning by these tools.

Notes

1 Flavell, J. H. (1979). Metacognition and cognitive monitoring: A new area of cognitive–developmental inquiry. *American Psychologist, 34*(10), 906–911. https://doi.org/10.1037/0003-066X.34.10.906
2 Open Science Framework link to materials and data from Morey et al. 2025. https://osf.io/m8ks4/overview
3 Morey, C. C., AuBuchon, A. M., Attwood, M., Castelain, T., Cowan, N., Crepaldi, D., Fjerdingstad, E., Fredriksen, E., Jarrold, C., Koch, C., Lelonkiewicz, J. R., Lupyan, G., Mendenhall, W., Moreau, D., Schonberg, C., Tamnes, C. K., Vlach, H. & Elliott E. M. (2025). Is verbal rehearsal strategic? An investigation into overt rehearsal of nameable pictures in 5- to 10-year-old children. *Journal of Cognition and Development*, DOI: 10.1080/15248372.2024.2389123
4 Coffman, J. L., Westover, A. E., Grammer, J. K., McNeish, D. & Ornstein, P. A. (2025). Deliberate memory strategy development: The interplay of children's self-regulated learning abilities and teachers' cognitive processing language. *Journal of Applied Research in Memory and Cognition*. https://doi.org/10.1037/mac0000241
5 Oana, O. & Flavia, P. (2025). The meta-intelligent child: Validating the MKIT as a tool to develop metacognitive knowledge in early childhood. *Journal of Intelligence, 13*(11), 149. https://doi.org/10.3390/jintelligence13110149
6 Kubota, M., Hadley, L. V., Schaeffner, S., Könen, T., Meaney, J.-A., Morey, C. C., Auyeung, B., Moriguchi, Y., Karbach, J. & Chevalier, N. (2023). The effect of metacognitive executive function training on children's executive function, proactive control, and academic skills. *Developmental Psychology, 59*(11), 2002–2020. https://doi.org/10.1037/dev0001626
7 Dangol, A., Zhao, R., Wolfe, R., Ramanan, T., Kientz, J. A. & Yip, J. (2025). "AI just keeps guessing": Using ARC puzzles to help children identify reasoning errors in generative AI. In *Proceedings of the 24th Interaction Design and Children* (pp. 444–464). https://doi.org/10.1145/3713043.3728836

Part III

Myths, Truths, and Final Conclusions

Chapter 8

Myths About Memory and Attention

In this chapter, I will discuss a number of myths about memory and learning.

Humans Only Use 10 Per Cent of the Brain[1]

This is a myth and it is not correct. We use all the parts of our brains at different times, awake or asleep. When we dream, the brain is even more active than when we are awake. My colleague, Heather Lucas, makes a good point about brain functions. She says: "neurons require a constant supply of oxygen and energy to remain alive and functional, so essentially all brain tissue is metabolically active all the time"[2].

It seems no one is sure where this myth originated, but it has persisted for over a century. It is discussed in a book on myths in the field of psychology by Dr Lilienfeld and his colleagues[3], and in other sources like the website Neuroscience for Kids[4]. Does the myth suggest that young children use even less than 10 per cent of memory because they are younger and have poorer memory abilities than young adults? This idea is untrue and should be dismissed.

One possibility is that this 10 per cent myth originated in the fact that brain functions are specialized. For example, we know that there are portions of the brain, particularly in the left hemisphere for most right-handed people, that specialize in the comprehension of speech. However, because some areas of the brain are devoted to speech comprehension does not mean that they are the only ones active when someone is talking. Understanding how we take in sights and sounds from the environment and translate those environmental signals into a format that the brain can use (i.e., transduction) is the first step. We can then follow the signals to the relevant processing areas of the brain, and finally to a response. This pathway illustrates the many neural structures and functions that are involved in everyday interactions.

Take a conversation as an example. You receive visual input from the shape of the person's mouth when they pronounce different words, and this visual input is combined with the sounds of the language. After the signals reach

DOI: 10.4324/9781003672814-11

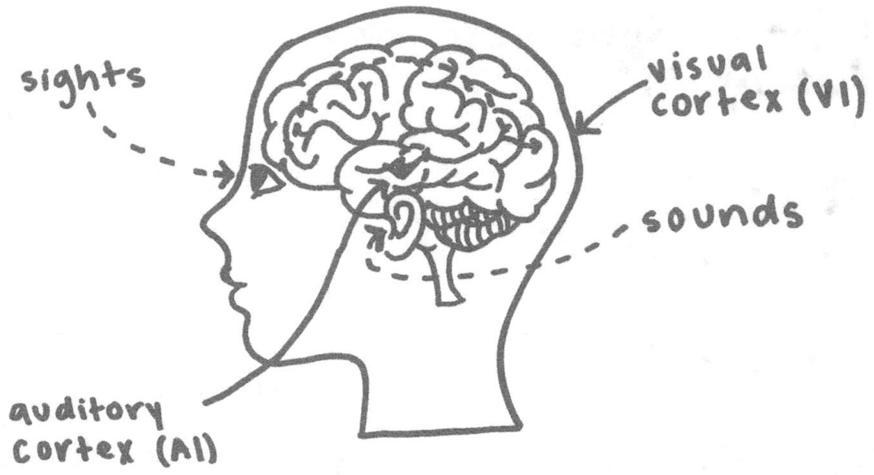

Figure 8.1 The multiple steps of processing involved during a conversation. The visual images are encoded and processed by the visual area of the brain, starting in VI in the occipital lobes. At the same time, the sounds are processed through the ears and into the auditory cortex of the brain (AI), located in the temporal lobes. Other brain areas, not depicted here, are involved in decoding the larger context, individual word meanings, and the possible emotional content of the conversation.

your eyes and ears, they are translated from the physical form of light waves and sound waves by specialized cells that turn the physical energy into neural energy. Then the sights and sounds go to the first processing area for each sense, the visual cortex (VI) and the auditory cortex (AI). Next, the information is compared to information already stored in memory and, finally, a response is prepared. Signals are sent to the motor cortex to prepare your spoken response (see Figure 8.1). This example is an oversimplification of these complex neural processes, but my point is that even seemingly everyday functions like responding to someone in a conversation are multifaceted and require the interaction of multiple brain areas. The very idea that so many steps could be happening but that we only use 10 per cent of our brain to accomplish them is not realistic.

Right-Brained Versus Left-Brained

In a different yet related myth, people talk about someone being "left-brained" or "right-brained". While different aspects of function are connected to certain brain areas, we use all of our brain over time. This idea was originally popularized as a rationale for individual differences, such as those who are more visual and artistic (i.e., right-brained) compared to those who are skilled with words (i.e., left-brained). However, this classification is another example of an oversimplification and misunderstanding of research findings. When I discuss the basics of brain anatomy and functioning in Chapter 2, I mention the two hemispheres of the brain and the organization of the left and right sides of the cortex. Yet saying someone **cannot** complete a task because they are a "right-brained person" is limiting their potential.

Again, the history of this myth is not known, but it may be related to asymmetries in functioning. One prominent example of asymmetry is handedness. Many more people are right-hand-dominant than left-hand-dominant. The finding that many language functions are located in the left hemisphere of the brain goes back to the 1860s when a French doctor named Paul Broca[5] treated a patient with damage to the left hemisphere, which severely limited his ability to produce speech. He was referred to as "Tan" because although he could understand speech, when he tried to respond he could only generate the word "tan". Research in this area led to major developments in the understanding of speech disorders, such as aphasia, that can occur after brain injury. However, it could also be why people later began to believe in the superiority of the left hemisphere over the right, because it was associated with language and logic. The right hemisphere was associated with being left-handed, and with the functions of spatial reasoning and creativity.

In the 1950s, while much more was known about brain structure and function than in the 1860s, much was yet to be discovered. During this time, doctors and scientists were trying to improve the lives of people with severe epilepsy, a condition that can lead to seizures. Some patients had such severe seizures that it was difficult or impossible for them to lead independent lives, hold down jobs, or drive a car. I discussed Henry Molaison earlier and the surgery that removed his hippocampus. A different surgery was developed to separate the left and right hemispheres of the brain to reduce the amount of electrical communication between them. This procedure was effective in reducing the symptoms of epilepsy, and patients regained some independence. It also created a unique opportunity for testing brain function and investigating the lateralization of function in brains that could not communicate across the two hemispheres. One of the pioneers in this area was Roger W. Sperry. He was awarded half of the 1981 Nobel Prize for Physiology and Medicine for his discoveries on hemispheric functions. The other half of the award was split by Hubel and Wiesel for their discovery of information processing in the visual system.

These two points in history may have contributed to the subsequent development and popularity of the myth that people can be categorized as "right-brained" or "left-brained"[6]. The notion was picked up in many aspects of education, including art education. I can remember as a child seeing a book called *Drawing on the Right Side of your Brain*, as my mother enjoyed visual art, drawing, and painting. This book by Betty Edwards was published in 1979 and later reprinted in multiple editions, with the fourth published in 2012[7]. Thus, the idea that the right hemisphere had to be emphasized to engage creativity or artistic capacities of individuals was widespread, but the truth is that creativity is a product of both hemispheres. Language is located mostly on the left, but some aspects of understanding humor and other practical uses of language involve the right hemisphere.

Research has demonstrated that as children grow into adulthood, language becomes increasingly more lateralized to the left hemisphere in most people. However, this is not true for everyone. Right-handed children are more likely to have language structures and functions in the left hemisphere of the brain. In one study, left-handed children were given brain scans to determine if their language structures and functions were localized in the same manner[8], and some differences emerged. While most of the left-handed children showed left-hemisphere language lateralization, some showed evidence of right hemisphere language lateralization. While these findings can tell us about brain activity in the moment, it is harder to understand what they may mean in terms of real-world behaviors. I interpret them to mean that it is important not to overgeneralize and overapply research findings, but to remember that there can be nuances and individual differences in the way that people function in daily life.

Listening To Classical Music Such as Mozart Can Make You Smarter

Like the myth that we only use 10 per cent of our brains, the idea that listening to a particular type of music can make a person smarter has a certain appeal. Could we be "smarter" if we used 100 per cent of our brains? Well, since we do use 100 per cent of our brains over time and in different tasks, we know this is not true. There is also extensive research into listening to music, and the bottom line seems to be that while it is good for many things, like improving your mood, there is no empirical evidence that it changes your cognitive function in a sustained way over time. Thus, in short, the answer to the question "can listening to music make you smarter?" is no.

One reason this myth has persisted may be due to a study on music listening and test performance[9] that received widespread media attention, surprising even the study's lead author, Dr Francis Rauscher[10]. In one of the experimental conditions, college students were asked to listen to ten minutes of a piece by Mozart and then take a spatial reasoning test. This is part of a larger battery of tests that measure someone's intelligence quotient, or IQ. (A spatial reasoning test is like Tetris™, which asks the player to manipulate a shape in their mind. There are other examples, like folding and cutting paper, that require imagining the outcome of a shape change or movement change). The other experimental conditions used by Dr Rauscher included silence and relaxation instructions (i.e., someone speaking in a relative monotone). The students who heard Mozart first and then took the spatial reasoning test performed better than the control group. The increase in spatial IQ scores after listening to ten minutes of a Mozart sonata was picked up by the media, with varying results. In short, the outcome of the study was exaggerated and misinterpreted, leading to broad social and commercial effects that were not always positive.

Keep in mind that the original study was conducted on a small group of college students, which as a group are not necessarily representative of the general population. The media linked the outcomes from this study to the idea that babies could become smarter if they were simply exposed to Mozart's music at an early age. The idea was further promoted when the Governor of Georgia at the time, Zell Miller, included funding in the state's budget to give each newborn child either a cassette tape or a CD of Mozart's music. Further, an entrepreneurial parent, Julie Aigner-Clark, started a company that produced books, videos, CDs, and other items for introducing babies to classical music to make them smarter. The product was called "Baby Einstein" . We owned many "Baby Einstein" VHS tapes and played them in the background when our daughters were young. These products became so popular that the company was eventually sold to Disney, and a long-running cartoon was created. It seems hard to believe that all of this could emerge from one research study with a small number of participants.

Where is the "Mozart Effect" today? Scientists have attempted to replicate the findings in many subsequent studies. Replication is an important component of the scientific process, as a successful replication can indicate that the findings of a study are not an anomaly, or that they did not happen by chance. The bottom line of this research is that while listening to Mozart is not a bad thing, it is not linked to a causal change in intelligence. Listening to music can increase arousal, or the overall level of a person's awareness and focus on a task. This change in arousal can be created by multiple sources and is not unique to listening to Mozart[11]. The "Mozart Effect" is a cautionary tale about jumping to conclusions without enough evidence to support those conclusions.

One element of conducting scientific research is considering the weight of evidence for particular findings, as opposed to studying them only in binary terms, such as being right or wrong. Researchers allow for conclusions to be qualified and updated when new information becomes available. In this case, it seems that the public policy intentions were good: it is understandable that researchers and a state-level government would want to improve outcomes for children. Unfortunately, the results that accumulated over time indicated that simply listening to Mozart was not the solution they had hoped it would be.

Learning Music Gives a Cognitive Advantage

What about the idea that music training can make someone smarter[12]? It is a related idea but asks a different question. Parents typically want the best for their children, and providing music lessons may be one way to give them a cognitive advantage – or is it? Research investigating the relationship between music training and intelligence has evolved over several decades. In the early

2000s it seemed the idea that "music makes you smarter" had empirical support. But many early studies used small sample sizes and inconsistent methodologies, making it difficult to form strong conclusions.

Where do things stand today? The evidence suggests that providing music lessons to a developing child will not lead to substantive changes in their cognitive function[13]. Nonetheless, it is still a wonderful way to teach children numerous skills and to build their self-confidence. I enrolled all three of my children in piano lessons to help them to reach these personal goals and found it to be a wonderful experience overall. My aim was to help to create confident and well-rounded children, and not necessarily to increase their overall cognitive function. The benefits of music instruction are numerous, and I could write another entire chapter about the ways that music can enrich our lives; however, as I have said for other topics, that is beyond the scope of this book.

Multiple peer-reviewed publications have addressed the relationship of musical training and short-term memory ability[14], executive functions[15], and general fluid intelligence[16]. Overall, these studies have found that those with more musical training outperform those without it, but the difference between the two groups is small. The most consistent findings indicate that musicians do better on musical memory tasks than non-musicians. This outcome is not surprising; it is like saying that someone who knows how to play tennis will do better on the tennis court than someone who does not. What is more interesting is whether learning to play music creates benefits in other areas of life, such as math or reading abilities. So far, that does not seem to be the case.

However, the causal direction of any cognitive benefits of learning music is still being investigated. Most prior studies did not use experimental designs of musical training that included active control groups, for example, in children[17]. Just as with the work on "brain training" that I discuss next, the design of a research study must be considered. Does it have enough participants to detect an effect if one exists? Is there a control group that is given some kind of task? Without an active control group, it is difficult to rule out alternative explanations that could emerge from the data. Work continues in this area; however, the bottom line is that learning music is a wonderful thing to do even if you are not trying to improve your cognitive abilities. If you are interested in reading more about the wonderful ways that music is integrated into our lives, and the power of music to help us to remember moments from our past, I recommend Elizabeth Margulis' book, *Transported: The Everyday Magic of Musical Daydreams*[18].

Brain Training Programs Change Intellectual Functioning and Make a Person Smarter

I am skeptical about companies offering products to improve cognitive functioning. I believe that "If something sounds too good to be true, it probably is". I would be delighted if there were easy fixes to dramatically improve people's memory functioning; however, this is a case where optimism alone is not enough. Decades of research have demonstrated that the concept of "brain training" in a general sense is not successful. I talk about this briefly in Chapter 5.

Let me begin with some definitions. "Brain training" in scientific literature is mostly discussed in terms of a general type of cognitive training or, as mentioned above, as a more specific example such as math training or working memory training. The more specific examples focus more narrowly on a skillset or domain.

To discuss this more narrowly, we can use the term "**cognitive training**", which is a set of activities that build knowledge and skills in different types of cognitive tasks, such as memory or general intelligence. One definition is: "*Cognitive training* refers to interventions using cognitive tasks or intellectually demanding activities, the goal of which is to enhance general cognitive ability"[19] As discussed above, learning music with the goal of improving overall speed of thinking, memory, and cognition is an example of cognitive training. However, learning music with the goal of getting better at a musical instrument is a specific type of training with the result being "near transfer". **Near transfer** occurs when a person learns and practices a task or skill and then improves in the performance of either that task or something very similar. This can be contrasted with **far transfer**, which is often the goal of cognitive training. Far transfer is seen when someone learns a particular set of skills, such as performing working memory tasks, and then improves in an unrelated skill such as a measure of general intelligence. Going back to the idea of music training, if far transfer effects are consistently found, this is solid evidence that learning to play a musical instrument leads to improvements in other domains such as general intelligence. The bulk of the data does not support this conclusion (as discussed in the section on children taking music lessons).

Another term that is important to mention here is **placebo effect**. This can be defined as "people's expectations or beliefs influencing or determining their experience in a given situation."[20] Research has shown that these effects can be powerful and must be taken into consideration when designing and conducting an intervention study. For example, if a study supposedly provides evidence that a cognitive training program, or over-the-counter memory supplement, can improve cognition or memory in the long term, it is important to determine if the researchers controlled for placebo effects. There are multiple ways to do this, including keeping both the participants and the researchers unaware of which experimental groups or conditions they are in (known as a double-blind experiment). Controlling for placebo effects is also a common practice in clinical trials testing the effectiveness of new medications, for example. In addition to considering whether the researchers controlled for placebo effects, it is important to consider the source of the study. Was it conducted by the company itself, and/or were the researchers funded by the company? Considering the source is a good way to apply a critical lens to the review of research outcomes.

Returning to the idea of cognitive training in general: several studies have examined whether true improved cognition can result from cognitive training interventions. Gobet and Sala[29] discuss the benefits of meta-analysis and what can be learned from the outcomes of meta-analytic techniques. Meta-analysis is discussed in Chapter 5 in relation to research on ADHD and working memory. In summary, it is a method of compiling published research to assess the strength of the evidence for a particular conclusion. In the case of cognitive training, the key outcome is to demonstrate far transfer and a true effect that shows a reliable difference between a control group and the cognitive intervention group. The goal of this research is to demonstrate that cognitive interventions lead to lasting improvements in cognitive functioning, again going beyond specific tasks that may have been a part of the training. The data do not support this conclusion. While near transfer effects are often found, far transfer effects are not. If a person wants to get better at math, specific training in math tasks can lead to improvements. However, if a person wants to improve overall cognitive functioning, training in cognitive tasks alone does not appear to be the answer.

Learning Styles

It is not true that children have one specific learning style, such as being a visual or an auditory learner. This myth can be harmful if someone thinks they "cannot learn" because the teaching method is inconsistent with their perceived learning style[21]. If a teacher uses a written method to teach a child who believes they are an "auditory learner", then the child may believe that they cannot be successful because their learning style does not match the mode of delivery. There is no evidence that such learning styles exist[22], yet this myth is persistent, difficult to eradicate, and harmful to parents, teachers, and children[23].

As with the 10 per cent myth, it is not clear how this myth originated. It was popularized in the 1980s and many educators and parents still believe it, despite it being untrue. Substantive empirical evidence questioning the strict interpretation of this view is summarized effectively by Pashler and colleagues. If an auditory learner was able to retain new information most effectively when it was delivered in the auditory modality, such as the teacher giving verbal descriptions or playing an audio recording of a lecture, then they would score more highly in tests than a student who was "mismatched" with their learning style. This mismatch could occur, for example, if an auditory learner was shown information in the form of diagrams, pictures, or other purely visual content. The evidence does not support this view. Children and adults can and do learn from more than one modality.

This myth may persist because the concept of learning something best in one particular format resonates with people's individual experiences. Meeting someone for the first time and learning their name, for example, may be easier for some people if the name is spoken. Others may feel it is easier if there are nametags and they can see the name written. The research findings suggest that the combination of seeing the person's name and hearing it leads to the most persistent learning. The evidence for this "combination effect" is synthesized and reviewed in the work by Mayer on the Cognitive Theory of Multimedia Learning[24]. Thus, while we may have preferences, it is possible for people to learn new information even when it is presented in a modality that may seem counter to their own learning preferences.

Another bit of evidence that is problematic for this view is that the subject matter may determine which modality is best for effective and efficient learning. Many people have tried to learn a new language, a skill that involves both auditory and visual modalities. On the other hand, learning to draw or paint involves both motor skills, such as how to hold a paintbrush, and visual skills. Listening to someone explaining the most effective way to paint may not the best way to learn. People have preferences for how they take in new information and certain material may be better suited to some approaches than others. Children can learn in different formats and should be encouraged to learn in multiple modalities. Material that lends itself to interaction and physical manipulation, such as the fundamental principles of physics, is more engaging when children can involve their auditory, visual, and kinesthetic senses. However, it is myth to suggest that a child **cannot** learn without a match between the delivery of the content and their preferred modality.

Attention has a "span", and It Is Getting Shorter Due To Technology/ Social Media[25]

Part of the reason this myth persists is imprecise terminology. A cognitive psychologist may interpret the meaning of "attention span" differently to a layperson. I discuss the meaning of the term "span" in Chapter 3 on the limits of short-term memory.

Besides terminology and the potential confusion it may cause, many people are concerned that reduced attention span is due to changes in the brain. However, the type of changes that would have to be involved here would take a very long time. An alternative interpretation is that people are now less willing to devote significant focused attention to any one source or activity without attention switches or other forms of multi-tasking. To put it in terms used by Michelle Miller, people have lowered their tolerance for boredom[26]. Thus, if we push people to the limit of how long they could maintain attention on one task without switching their focus, we can estimate the maximum length of focused attention. Prior research in this area has taken measurements of people at work or in other real-world or ecologically valid settings, which is very important. However, I believe it is a misnomer to call it a "span" measurement without pushing people to achieve the longest focus they can have on any one thing. Just because people choose to switch attention between a word-processing program and an email program does not mean that they are unable to maintain focus over a longer period. It suggests switching attention between tasks has become more common. Making people aware of these behaviors is important, because they can then develop strategies to avoid switching frequently. Psychologists are trying to communicate the costs of task switching to help people sustain their focus and get more done efficiently[27]. Besides trying to focus exclusively on one task at a time, there are other ways to combat distraction and avoid multi-tasking, which I revisit in Chapter 9.

Your Brain can Get "full"

As I discuss in Chapter 4, long-term memory may be unlimited. Where did this myth originate? As with the others discussed in this chapter, it is not entirely clear. Being unable to retrieve a memory correctly and your brain being unable to take in new information are two different things. Sometimes doing hard mental work is tiring. People can feel fatigued without necessarily doing anything physical. Perhaps the connection between hard mental work, fatigue, and a desire to sleep has contributed to the idea that after a particularly long day, or a long study session, the brain is full. This is not true. However, it does remind us of the importance of getting good sleep. That topic is discussed in Chapter 9.

Scientists have attempted to quantify exactly how much information the brain can store. The methodology is based on comparing the ways computers store information and the way the brain stores information, as discussed in Chapter 3 in the section on analogies. Computers code information in binary terms, 1s and 0s, or "bits". Scientists translated the neuronal connections to estimate the number of bits that one synaptic connection could hold[28]. This process involved using a small area of hippocampal brain tissue and careful measurements to determine the synapses and the strength of the connection: the result was 4.7 bits. If one knew exactly how many connections existed, precise estimations could be made.

These individual units of information are then measured in "bytes", which are eight bits. I have seen websites suggesting we have a capacity of 2.5 million gigabytes[29] (a gigabyte is 1,000,000 bytes) and the amount of information that our brains can hold could be even larger. This large number is difficult to conceive. I mentioned this topic to my teenage son, who immediately said something about petabytes, which prompted me to do some more research to gain a better understanding of the terminology. It turns out that there is a scale of storage capacities that is built upon how much information is in a bit, and then a byte, and then up to the largest unit of measurement, which will probably continue to increase as technology improves in this area. In the early days of computing, I used a floppy disk to store a few files, and the capacity was 1.44 megabytes. I remember the exciting addition of the "zip disk", which was the equivalent of 10 floppy disks. It is almost laughable to think how small those storage limits were in relation to what is available today. To put the capacity in different terms, it would take about 694,445 floppy disks from the 1990s to equal 1 terabyte (1 TB).

Nonetheless, our brains can hold vast amounts of information, regardless of whether it is in terms of millions of gigabytes or petabytes. Additional research is continuing in this area[30] with the advantage of newer technologies, better imaging precision, and the assistance of AI to map neuronal networks that would take human researchers a very long time to accomplish without the aid of AI tools.

Another way to think about the capacity of the brain is to measure it in daily tasks. This research has ecological validity, or relevance to how people do things in the real world, compared to work that is conducted purely in the lab without direct reference to daily living. Scientists were interested in the capacity of long-term memory and how to measure the limits[31]. They showed participants 2500 pictures, presented for three seconds each. The viewing took place over several hours. Afterwards, they were presented with pairs of images and asked to indicate which one that had seen before (is it old or is it new?), which is a standard way to assess recognition memory. When participants were shown an old picture in a pair with a new picture, their ability to correctly recognize the old picture was a staggering 92 per cent correct!

Memory Is in One "Spot" in the Brain

This myth is grounded in brain anatomy; however, it represents a misunderstanding of the numerous networks of neurons and connections across multiple areas of the brain. Research with both human and non-human animals has helped us to understand the vital role that the hippocampus plays in memory formation. Nonetheless, retrieval of stored memories relies on more than any one element of anatomy or any one brain location.

As I discuss in the topic of the 10 per cent myth, many parts of the brain are involved in even simple tasks. Memories are created by the involvement of multiple senses; thinking about the way the house smells when you first walk into your grandmother's home during the holidays can invoke multiple aspects of your memory. You will engage your visual memories of the way the house looks with the holiday decorations, as well as the auditory memories of the holiday music playing in the background. I have discussed the idea that memories are reconstructions of prior events that engage multiple networks in the brain. If viewed through that lens, it becomes clear that memories are multi-sensory and cannot be stored in only one location. A myth like this works well when writing a script and lies behind inaccurate depictions of memory functioning in television dramas and movies.

A movie that displayed the idea of keeping all your cognitive functions intact but erasing your memory of a specific person was *Eternal Sunshine of the Spotless Mind*. Movies like this may contribute to myths about how memory works. (Spoiler alert: if you have not seen this movie, then skip this section and move on to the next myth.) In the movie, the main characters had been in a relationship that had ended badly. The characters were presented with the opportunity to selectively erase the memories of any interactions and shared experiences from their relationship, while leaving all other aspects of their memory functions intact. The hypothetical technology in the movie displayed images of brain scans with certain locations lighting up in response to the experience of a memory of the relationship. The technicians from the memory erasure company could then selectively erase the memory so that the main characters would no longer feel sad that the relationship was over or be troubled by these memories. In a romantic twist, while the procedure is happening, the man in the relationship subconsciously decides he wants to mentally hide from the technicians so that he can preserve his memories of the woman and their time together. Ultimately, they find a way to each other and meet "for the first time" all over again. While the movie is not scientifically accurate, it brings up serious questions about the role of memories in defining who we are as people. It also highlights the close connections between our memories and our emotions. Nonetheless, because memories are broadly distributed across brain networks, this type of scenario is simply fiction.

Memory Works Like a Recording Device and Plays Back an Exact Copy of Prior Experiences

This myth suggests that it would not be possible to "misremember" or confuse the details of an event. We know that is not true. As discussed in Chapters 1 and 2, memory is reconstructive and each time we retrieve a memory we are essentially "rebuilding it" from our neuronal networks. We can have strong confidence that our memories are accurate, unfortunately, even when the details of the memory are not correct[32]. Like the myth above, this one has been reinforced in movies as well. However, because our memories are created through connections of neurons and the interaction of multiple networks, they are rebuilt through patterns of neuronal firing. The gist of the memory is maintained, but small details may get changed in the retelling. Then, the next time a memory is recalled, the memories of the prior retelling are also incorporated, which can lead to continued shifts over time. I suspect that neurotruth is harder to incorporate into the storyline of a movie, which is why it is more common to see a character play back exactly what happened in the past.

Researchers have studied the inaccuracies of memory recall and have helped the field to understand the ways in which similar material can be confused. Furthermore, research has shown that people can recall words from a list that were not actually on the list. We sometimes talk about this as a "false memory". Because we often associate words and facts with similar ideas, a list of words can be created that share a general theme, such as words that relate to the idea of "sleep" but do not contain the word "sleep". However, without ever seeing the word itself, participants in research studies presented with such a list have recalled being shown the word "sleep". They can accurately recall words such as "bed", "pillow", "dream", etc. but it becomes difficult to remember whether the word "sleep" was in the list because of its high level of association with the other words. While warning participants about this false recall can reduce the effect, it was still not eliminated[33].

This memory paradigm of using associated word lists has also been tested in children, and the researchers were careful to use words in the vocabulary of younger children such as 2nd graders. The younger children in the study showed lower rates of false recall than the older children and adults, indicating a different strategic approach to remembering the word lists. The older children, 5th and 8th graders, showed a developmental transition that indicated a heavier reliance on their semantic networks (i.e., related facts and words), which in turn led to more adult-like levels of false recall[34]. Questions about the way that children rely on their semantic networks and the ways in which memory errors can change with development continue to be investigated and are critical for our understanding of children's memory development[35].

These facts about how memory retrieval works are important for learning new material and have implications for the classroom. If the specific details are critically important, then the strategies that a person will use to encode, maintain, and retrieve that information can focus on exact answers, such as repeatedly reviewing questions and answers until a criterion can be reached. The more cues that are created around the details, the more successful the retrieval. Also, repeated practice over a longer time will lead to longer-lasting memories, as opposed to "cramming". I discuss these strategies in more detail in Chapter 9. But if a person believes that memory works like the camera on their phone, they may be less inclined to put in the effort that is needed for successful and accurate retrieval. They may also not understand the ways in which similar things can be confused in the recall process. Thus, understanding these myths is important to make the most of someone's memory functioning.

With Technology, There Is No Need to Memorize Anything Anymore

I have heard parents say something similar to this "memorizing myth". However, there are times and situations when having a baseline of knowledge that can be quickly and easily accessed by the cognitive system is a big benefit.

In the 5th grade, I had a propensity to talk a lot in school. My teacher disapproved and devised a strategy to help me to curtail my verbosity: I had to write out all 12 times tables 12 times each. My memory of this is of a unique torture that she had devised to keep her students in line. However, I have often been grateful for this memorization task because I can still quickly and accurately calculate these values in my head. Thank you, Mrs George.

Memorization is one of the concepts presented in Bloom's taxonomy[36]. This taxonomy is often presented in the form of a pyramid, with the "lower levels" of learning at the bottom (see Figure 8.2), forming the base. It was originally proposed in 1956 and underwent revision in 2001[37]. The visual analogy of the pyramid is a very apt one for teaching new concepts. Beginning with the basics like definitions and **memorizing** the core facts, children can begin to **understand** new material, which is the next level. Deeper **comprehension** is based on knowing the general idea of a concept before it can be **applied** and **reasoned** about.

I learned about this first-hand when I gave an exam in Introduction to Psychology. One of my students asked me later why I gave such hard tests. I asked him to clarify because it had not been my intention to trick anyone or make things unnecessarily difficult. He explained that all his tests in high school were primarily definitions and learning to match the names of people with the year of their work, or the event in history with the date. My tests, he said, asked him to apply the knowledge, such as coming to a conclusion after reading a scenario and then answering questions about it.

This interaction showed me that not every learner is taught to engage with their course materials at different levels. Moving up the pyramid takes the learner into application of the concepts. But before you can apply new

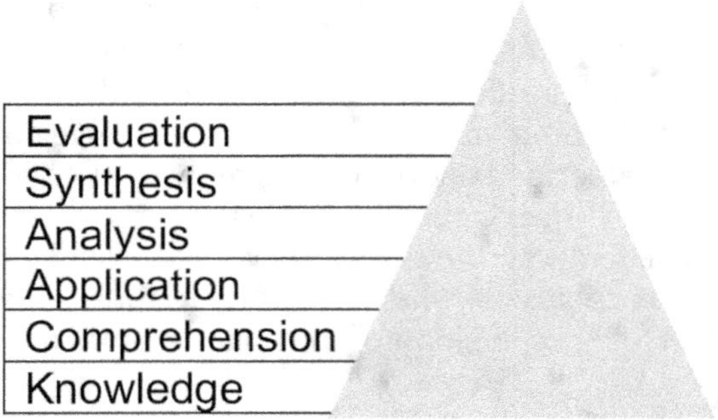

Figure 8.2 The original version of Bloom's Taxonomy (1956) illustrating the different levels of learning that occur when a person first encounters new information and must gain new knowledge. The framework depicts moving up the levels of the taxonomy to illustrate deeper processing, application, and the ability to critique the new information.

knowledge, it must have a place in your mind with the correct vocabulary. My student was skilled in the lowest levels of the taxonomy, but he had not had practice moving up to the higher levels of reasoning. I realized I could use Bloom's taxonomy in my teaching. If I wanted my students to move up the levels of the pyramid, my course design needed to show explicitly how learning could be assessed at different levels. I started including more practice in the classroom, with scenarios and vignettes, so that the students learned how to move beyond memorization into deeper levels of thinking.

Continuing up the pyramid requires the learner to analyze the material. There are many effective tools for encouraging analysis, including asking students to compare two concepts, or to discover how a new concept may relate to content that was covered earlier in the course. Helping students to make connections across different chapters, for example, or even across different courses, can show them that much of what they are learning overlaps. But this must be explained to the students; they are less likely to see it on their own. To help students move up the levels of learning, scaffolding and practice must be provided in the classroom.

The final two levels of the pyramid are associated with the highest level of understanding, in a way that I think of as internalizing the knowledge. Students can reflect upon the information, apply it to new situations, solve problems and create new solutions. I do not expect beginning college students to move all the way up the pyramid in one semester. But over the course of multiple semesters and being exposed to the same concepts across different courses and different scenarios, the students gain the tools to assess their own learning and apply their skills in unique ways. Talking to students about these different levels of learning is one way to help them to reach the ultimate goal: learning how to learn, no matter what the content.

I did not learn about the usefulness and the application of Bloom's Taxonomy when studying to become a cognitive psychologist; I learned it through my interactions with the Teaching for Learning Center at the University of Missouri in Columbia, Missouri. For many years, the disciplines of education and cognitive psychology were not directly connected. Fortunately, through the work of many engaged scholars from both fields, we are beginning to see a greater integration and interest in having joint conversations about how to help students succeed in the classroom[38].

Now I am teaching Introduction to Statistics to college students. This course has illustrated the effectiveness of Bloom's taxonomy to me from a teaching perspective. It helps to think about action verbs that can be connected to the learning objectives in a course. Using this framework helps me to move away from asking too many "low-level" questions like simply recalling knowledge and not enough questions and course activities that encourage deeper learning. Additionally, there are several recommendations for directly talking to children and college students about the general concepts represented in Bloom's taxonomy. As discussed in Chapter 7 on metamemory, to increase self-regulation of learning and reflection on one's own learning (e.g., metacognition[39]), learners must understand that simple memorization is only useful up to a point. It will not lead to the deeper levels of connection and conceptual understanding that higher levels of the taxonomy, such as analyzing and evaluating, will create.

Take-Away Points

Myths discussed in this chapter:

- Humans only use 10 per cent of the brain. Not true! At any given time, you are using multiple parts of your brain. All the parts are relevant for actions in a variety of settings and for maintaining different aspects of cognitive and bodily functioning.
- Listening to classical music such as Mozart can make you smarter. While this idea seems very appealing, it is also not true. Music can do many wonderful things, but it is unlikely to lead to deep changes in someone's cognitive functioning.
- Brain training programs truly change your intellectual functioning and make a person smarter overall. What we know to be true is that practicing a particular task or skill over time will lead to improvement. This transfer of knowledge from one similar type of skill to another is called near transfer. It is much harder to find clear evidence of far transfer, or receiving training in one skill or ability that then carries over to something quite different.
- Children have one specific learning style, such as being a visual or an auditory learner. As with the idea of brain training programs, there is no clear evidence that this is true. Children can learn in multiple ways and may show preferences but are basically amazing learning machines. Why limit them?
- Attention has a "span", and it is getting shorter. While there is anecdotal evidence to support this idea, it is more likely that the rapid changes in technology have changed our tolerance for sitting quietly or just being bored. When motivated and interested, children can devote their attention to a task over time.
- Your brain can get full. While doing a cognitively demanding task can make you feel tired, it is highly unlikely that the brain can ever get so filled with information that we are unable to take in any new facts or ideas. The storage capacity of the human brain is quite large.
- Memory is in one spot in the brain. While we know that certain areas of the brain are extremely important for memory, like the hippocampus, memories are multifaceted and are located across distributed neuronal networks. They are not like a file in a file drawer.

- Memory works like a recording device and plays back an exact copy of prior experiences. If this were true, it would not be possible to remember something incorrectly or to ask someone to repeat something. Children may be accused of not listening or not paying attention (which can happen), but it may be that they were distracted or just overloaded and could not remember all the details. Since memory does not work like a recording device, and children have smaller memory capacities than adults, it is important to work with them using age-appropriate memory expectations.
- With technology today, there is no need to memorize anything anymore. I agree that technology is very helpful in many settings, but it does not replace the need to learn basic facts and definitions. The foundation of learning starts with factual information. Having quick and easy access to facts and definitions, such as multiplication tables, can be very useful in life.

Chapter Summary

Myths about the brain and about memory, sometimes also called neuromyths, cause confusion and misunderstandings about brain function. If we believe something untrue about the way that memory or attention work, we may take actions that are not beneficial or could hinder successful cognition. Children learn, grow, and develop cognitive functions rapidly, and exposing them to myths about their memory and attention systems could lead to negative outcomes. It is important to empower children to learn about their own memory and attention, and by understanding neuro-truths as opposed to neuromyths, they can make better decisions about their own learning.

Notes

1 Chew, S. L. (August 29, 2018). Myth: We only use 10% of our brains. www.psychologicalscience.org/uncategorized/myth-we-only-use-10-of-our-brains.html
2 Lucas, H. D. (2026). Personal communication on May 19.
3 Lilienfeld, S. O., Lynn, S. J., Ruscio, J., & Beyerstein, B. L. (2010). *50 great myths of popular psychology: Shattering widespread misconceptions about human behavior.* Wiley Blackwell.
4 Chudler, E. H. (retrieved August 3, 2026) Neuroscience for kids. https://faculty.washington.edu/chudler/tenper.html
5 Pessoa, L. & Hof, P. R. (2015). From Paul Broca's great limbic lobe to the limbic system. *The Journal of Comparative Neurology, 523*(17), 2495–2500. https://doi.org/10.1002/cne.23840
6 Corballis, M. C. (2014). Left brain, right brain: facts and fantasies. *PLoS Biology, 12*(1), e1001767. https://doi.org/10.1371/journal.pbio.1001767
7 Edwards, B. (2012). *Drawing on the right side of the brain.* Penguin.

8 Szaflarski, J. P., Rajagopal, A., Altaye, M., Byars, A. W., Jacola, L., Schmithorst, V. J. ... & Holland, S. K. (2012). Left-handedness and language lateralization in children. *Brain Research, 1433*, 85–97. https://doi.org/10.1016/j.brainres.2011.11.026
9 Rauscher, F. H., Shaw, G. L. & Ky, K. N. (1993). Music and spatial task performance. *Nature, 365*(6447), 611. https://doi.org/10.1038/365611a0
10 Spiegel, A. (June 28, 2010). National Public Radio, Morning Edition. www.npr.org/2010/06/28/128104580/mozart-effect-was-just-what-we-wanted-to-hear
11 Gray, C. & Sergio, D. S. (2007). The Mozart effect: it's time to face the music!, in Della Sala, S. (ed.), *Tall tales about the mind and brain: Separating fact from fiction* (Oxford, online edition, March 22 2012). https://doi.org/10.1093/acprof:oso/9780198568773.003.0011
12 Schellenberg, E. G. (2004). Music lessons enhance IQ. *Psychological Science, 15*(8), 511–514. https://doi.org/10.1111/j.0956-7976.2004.00711.x
13 Schellenberg, E. G. (2020). Music training, individual differences, and plasticity. In M. S. C. Thomas, D. Mareschal & I. Dumontheil (Eds), *Educational Neuroscience: Development Across the Life Span* (pp. 415–441). Routledge/Taylor & Francis Group. https://doi.org/10.4324/9781003016830-21
14 Grassi, M, Talamini, F, Altoè, G. et al. (2025). Do musicians have better short-term memory than nonmusicians? A multilab study. *Advances in Methods and Practices in Psychological Science, 8*(4). https://doi.org/10.1177/25152459251379432
15 Slevc, L. R., Davey, N. S., Buschkuehl, M. & Jaeggi, S. M. (2016). Tuning the mind: Exploring the connections between musical ability and executive functions. *Cognition, 152*, 199–211. https://doi.org/10.1016/j.cognition.2016.03.017
16 Swaminathan, S., Schellenberg, E. G., & Khalil, S. (2017). Revisiting the association between music lessons and intelligence: Training effects or music aptitude? *Intelligence, 62*, 119–124. https://doi.org/10.1016/j.intell.2017.03.005
17 Sala, G. & Gobet, F. (2017). When the music's over. Does music skill transfer to children's and young adolescents' cognitive and academic skills? A meta-analysis. *Educational Research Review, 20,* 55–67. https://doi.org/10.1016/j.edurev.2016.11.005
18 Margulis, E. H. (2026). *Transported: The everyday magic of musical daydreams.* Liveright.
19 Gobet, F., & Sala, G. (2023). Cognitive training: A field in search of a phenomenon. *Perspectives on Psychological Science, 18*(1), 125–141. https://doi.org/10.1177/17456916221091830
20 Spielman, R. M., Jenkins, W. J., & Lovett, M. D. (2020). *Psychology 2e*. OpenStax.
21 American Psychological Association, press release (May 30, 2019). Belief in learning styles myth may be detrimental. www.apa.org/news/press/releases/2019/05/learning-styles-myth
22 Pashler, H., McDaniel, M., Rohrer, D. & Bjork, R. (2008). Learning styles: Concepts and evidence. *Psychological Science in the Public Interest, 9*(3),105–119. https://doi.org.10.1111/j.1539-6053.2009.01038.x
23 Sun X., Norton, O. & Nancekivell, S.E. (2023). Beware the myth: Learning styles affect parents', children's, and teachers' thinking about children's academic potential. *NPJ Science of Learning, 17,* 8(1):46. doi: 10.1038/s41539-023-00190-x. PMID: 37848467; PMCID: PMC10582039
24 Mayer, R.E. (2024). The past, present, and future of the Cognitive Theory of Multimedia Learning. *Educational Psychology Review, 36*(8). https://doi-org.libezp.lib.lsu.edu/10.1007/s10648-023-09842-1
25 American Psychological Association podcast, episode 225. Speaking of Psychology: Why our attention spans are shrinking, with Gloria Mark, PhD. www.apa.org/news/podcasts/speaking-of-psychology/attention-spans

26 Miller, M. D. (2022). *Remembering and forgetting in the age of technology: Teaching, learning, and the science of memory in a wired world*. West Virginia Press.
27 Mark, G. (2023). *Attention span: A groundbreaking way to restore balance, happiness and productivity*. Harlequin.
28 Bartol Jr., T. M., Bromer, C., Kinney, J., Chirillo, M. A., Bourne, J. N., Harris, K. M. & Sejnowski, T. J. (2015). Nanoconnectomic upper bound on the variability of synaptic plasticity. *Elife, 4*:e10778 https://doi.org/10.7554/eLife.10778
29 Reber, P. (May 1, 2010). What is the memory capacity of the human brain? www.scientificamerican.com/article/what-is-the-memory-capacity/
30 Sample, I. (May 9, 2024). Scientists find 57,000 cells and 150m neural connections in tiny sample of human brain. www.theguardian.com/science/article/2024/may/09/scientists-find-57000-cells-and-150m-neural-connections-in-tiny-sample-of-human-brain
31 Brady, T. F., Konkle, T., Alvarez, G. A. & Oliva, A. (2008). Visual long-term memory has a massive storage capacity for object details. *Proceedings of the National Academy of Sciences, 23,* 105(38),14325–9. https:/doi.org/10.1073/pnas.0803390105
32 Berkowitz, S. R., Garrett, B. L., Fenn, K. M. & Loftus, E. F. (2020). Convicting with confidence? Why we should not over-rely on eyewitness confidence. *Memory, 30*(1), 10–15. https://doi.org/10.1080/09658211.2020.1849308
33 Gallo, D. A., Roediger III, H. L. & McDermott, K. B. (2001). Associative false recognition occurs without strategic criterion shifts. *Psychonomic Bulletin & Review, 8*(3), 579–586. https://doi.org/10.3758/BF03196194
34 Metzger, R. L., Warren, A. R., Shelton, J. T., Price, J. & Reed, A. W. (2008). Do children 'DRM' like adults? False memory production in children. *Developmental Psychology, 44*(1), 169–181. https://doi.org/10.1037/0012-1649.44.1.169
35 Rousselle, M., Blaye, A. & Abadie, M. (2025). Development of false memories in 5- and 8-year-olds: The role of working memory maintenance mechanisms. *Journal of Experimental Child Psychology.* https://doi.org/10.1016/j.jecp.2025.106206
36 Bloom, B. S. (1956). *Taxonomy of educational objectives: The classification of educational goals Handbook I: Cognitive domain.* Longmans.
37 Anderson, L. W. & Krathwohl, D. R. et al. (Eds). (2001). *A taxonomy for learning, teaching, and assessing: A revision of Bloom's Taxonomy of Educational Objectives*. Allyn & Bacon (Pearson Education Group).
38 Agarwal, P. K. & Bain, P. M. (2024). *Powerful teaching: Unleash the science of learning*. John Wiley & Sons.
39 McGuire, S. Y. (2023). *Teach yourself how to learn: Strategies you can use to ace any course at any level*. Taylor & Francis.

Chapter 9

How Can I Improve My Memory and Attention?

One of my goals in writing this book is to empower people. Knowledge is an important tool, and I believe that as we use our memory and attention systems every day, we should know a bit more about how to make our cognitive systems operate at their highest level. This knowledge can help professionals in their own work and those who work with children to understand how memory and attention change and develop through childhood into adulthood. In this chapter, I discuss a variety of strategies that have been shown to be effective.

Use Multiple Modalities

You can learn in multiple modalities; why limit yourself to just one? Should a child learn primarily by reading or by listening? How about both? More exposure to the content through both the visual and auditory modalities, for example, means more cues will be created in memory and will provide more paths to successful retrieval. Chapters 2 and 3 describe how neurons and neural networks helped us to understand how our own brains work. This knowledge was leveraged to develop computers capable of learning (i.e., AI models). The power of networking neurons shows us that drawing on information in more than one modality can enhance our encoding of the information when we are learning it or hearing it or seeing it for the first time. The networks of the brain can work together to reconstruct the information when we need it.

Findings related to learning in more than one modality are not new. Cognitive psychologists have studied encoding, or how people initially take in and learn new information, since the early days of the discipline. One of the early studies on this topic was conducted in 1962 by Keppel and Underwood[1]. The researchers presented three letters to participants (such as, "k, q, f") and then had them wait through a three-second delay period during which they were asked to count backwards from a three-digit number. Imagine doing this task: you are given a three-letter item to remember and then a number such as 462 and asked to count backwards

DOI: 10.4324/9781003672814-12

from this number in increments of three (i.e., 462, 459, 456, etc.). Counting backwards is difficult and it was thought that participants would struggle to remember the letters. However, as I discuss in Chapter 6 on forgetting, proactive interference is reduced or eliminated when the material to be remembered is not too similar to the distractor. Thus, asking participants to remember letters while counting backwards with numbers should "protect" the memory trace from too much forgetting. People did very well on the first trial of this task.

In the second experiment in this series, the researchers presented the to-be-remembered items both visually and verbally. This presentation in two modalities boosted initial performance from around 80 per cent correct in Experiment 1 up to almost perfect performance in Experiment 2 on the first trial. This type of finding has been replicated in subsequent research conducted in Malaysia[2] and other countries. Replication, as mentioned in Chapter 8, is one way that scientists try to ensure the findings are significant and can be reproduced by other scientists in different labs with different participants. The replication showed that presenting stimuli visually and auditorily at the same time, compared to only verbally, or only in the auditory modality, led to a sizable increase in memory performance. The message here is: improving the way you initially "encode" or take in the information can make it easier to remember later, and that two modalities are better than one.

However, if someone shows visual information, such as words on a slide, and speaks about something other than what is shown on the screen, the conflict between the two sources of information is likely to cause the participant to switch their attention between the two sources. In a situation like this you might find yourself wondering "Should I listen to the speaker or should I read the words on the slide?". Switching attention rapidly between two types of modality is a less effective method of encoding than having consistent information presented in both modalities at the same time. Simplify the message by making it consistent between the modalities of presentation, and encoding will be more effective.

Believe That You Can Learn

While this may sound like an unusual recommendation, many students have said things to me like, "I'm just not good at math so therefore I can't do well in your statistics course." This type of self-defeating talk is an barrier that I must overcome to help this student. If a child is taught early on that they are "not good" at something, they are more likely to quit before really trying. One person who has been instrumental in delivering this message to children and college students is Saundra McGuire[3]. She started working with college students in chemistry classes and realized that this pattern of self-defeating self-talk was common. In the science, technology, engineering, and math (STEM) disciplines, the pressure to succeed is very high. Students from different backgrounds (such as being a member of an under-represented group or a first-generation college student) often struggle in these courses.

Saundra McGuire helped students understand the importance of metacognition, or learning about learning, that I covered in previous chapters. She has dedicated herself to helping students to identify what they did understand in the course content, and what they did not understand, so that they could better regulate their study time and study strategies. Importantly, she believes that each student is capable of learning, no matter how difficult the course. The testimonials of students who tell her how they changed their grades from a very low one to sometimes even an A are inspiring. Believing that you can learn is critical. Sometimes it just takes one other person to believe it in the first place, before a child or young adult can come around to that belief on their own.

Make Connections

Take the time to make things memorable by making connections to other ideas or related concepts (e.g., connecting something new to something students already know). At the risk of being repetitive, I want to remind everyone that knowing about neural networks also supports this point. Our brains work by comparing incoming information to existing information. If your cognitive system can use fewer resources to solve a problem, this is efficient and effective. We use the term "**cognitive economy**"; why make the brain networks work harder than they have to when solving a problem or learning new material? As we discussed in Chapter 8 (see myth #7), scientists have demonstrated that words are stored in the brain in connected semantic networks[4]. This research has made it clear that when we think about a word, such as "bird", we retrieve numerous concepts related to birds. Young children have fewer developed and connected semantic networks than older children and young adults[5]. As you can imagine, this is an area that continues to improve throughout life as people gain more experience and build their semantic networks. One of the benefits of older adulthood is having a robust vocabulary[6].

Being aware that children have a smaller vocabulary and less experience with words overall is helpful when teaching something new, especially to younger children. It boosts their understanding if the new material is related to something that they already know. Relating concepts can also increase a child's motivation to learn because it helps to ground the content in something that has meaning in the child's life. This concept is discussed in Chapter 4 on the connections between working memory and long-term memory. If you can pull information from your long-term memory system, it can help you to categorize, organize, or compare new details more quickly to something you already know. This connection between working memory and long-term memory can also help to bypass the limited capacity of working memory.

Connect the Content to Something Personal

Use emotion to your advantage. Current AI models cannot use this strategy, as the models do not currently have the capacity for emotion although new iterations of machine-learning models are trying to incorporate emotion-based responding. A full discussion of whether a computer program can ever emulate a full range of human emotions is beyond the scope of this book. As stated in the discussion of the hippocampus and the amygdala in Chapter 2, scientists know that emotions and memories are closely linked in humans (with an especially strong connection around the sense of smell).

One way that teachers can help students to harness the power of their emotions in learning is to introduce new material with connections their lives, as opposed to introducing a topic without a larger context. Tying in the emotions of surprise, amusement, and curiosity is critically important in engaging young learners (or indeed learners of any age). Author James Lang, in his book *Distracted,* compares teachers needing to capture the attention of their students with playwrights and movie producers[7]. The beginning of a play or the opening scenes of a movie are often filled with elements that lead to more questions. Writers and producers hope that, because of a sense of wonder and curiosity, fans will stick around and watch the full production or stay for the full movie.

Children do not have the large networks of knowledge that adults have but they do have emotions. Children actively build their networks through their experiences and exposure to new ideas and new content. Thus, it may seem obvious to adults how to make connections between learning something new and something that they already have experience with; but for children, these connections are less obvious. Reminding a child of something that they are particularly interested in, such as a book character that they admire or an artist whose music they really enjoy, can help them to make connections between their emotions and new content.

Use Visual and/or Auditory Imagery

Use visual imagery when learning something new to enhance the way you think about it. Research has shown that people can learn new information and retain it at higher levels when the information is shown in both picture and word format. This is known as the picture superiority effect and it has been studied in children and adults. In an early study on this topic[8], researchers presented sets of items either as words on a screen or as simple line drawings. Children were asked to remember the items later for a memory test. The children were in four age groups: seven to eight, eight to ten, 12–13, and 15–16 years of age. All the children showed that seeing items as pictures compared to words benefited their memory. Interestingly, the youngest children did not show as large a benefit; across the age groups, the picture superiority effect increased with age.

One of the theories behind this effect is that receiving information in multiple forms, such as in both pictures and words, can lead to dual coding[9] of the information. In other words, more ways of taking in the information in the first place can help to create more cues for later retrieval. More cues means that children are more likely to successfully recall what they need later.

Another way to leverage this information is to use imagery. Research using powerful imaging techniques to see which parts of the brain are active during different tasks has provided us with critical information about the power of using imagery. While not identical, areas of activation in the brain when doing visual imagery were similar to those activated when taking in visual information in real time[10]. Thus, thinking about something you are trying to remember and creating a visual image of it in your mind recruits similar brain areas as seeing it in the first place.

Get Good Sleep

Sleep helps the brain to organize information and to retain it. There is something called sleep-dependent memory consolidation that is important for our understanding of how sleep is beneficial for the creation and storage of memories in the brain. It is also related to how effectively retrieval can occur after learning something new[11]. Researchers have found clear evidence for a relationship between sleep, the hippocampus, and later memory performance. In general, there seems to be a more recent recognition of the major importance of sleep for overall health, wellness, and cognitive functioning[12]. We have always known that getting good sleep is important, but it is being studied and understood in new and improved ways that have clear implications for cognitive performance in children and adults.

An important aspect of studies on sleep is recognizing the ways that sleep patterns change over a lifespan. Younger children need more sleep than older children and adults to support their rapid learning and brain development. Recommendations vary by age[13]. For preschoolers aged three to five, the recommendation is ten to 13 hours, including naps. As children reach six to 12 years the recommendation is nine to 12 hours. Sleep patterns become more adult-like when children become adolescents, and the recommendation for ages 13–18 is eight to ten hours.

Young children especially benefit from night-time routines and predictable patterns that help them to transition to bedtime. Many parents know that this can be challenging, yet the importance of good sleep cannot be overstated. The benefits of bedtime routines extend beyond memory and cognition and include oral health by establishing good teeth-brushing habits, reading books for vocabulary development, and better emotion regulation. It is also important for children with ADHD to have bedtime routines, and there are checklists and other interventions to improve the sleep patterns of children with ADHD and other neurodevelopmental challenges[14].

Use Grouping and Acronyms

To memorize something, break it up into groups of items and/or make acronyms. Sing a song about it or write a poem about it – whatever makes the material more interesting. Songs contain several helpful structures that can boost memorization. They typically occur in a pattern and use elements like rhyming and repetition of important themes. These structures give the child a scaffold to support their memorization efforts.

The use of acronyms is also a well-known strategy. An acronym for learning the planets, such as My Very Excellent Mother Just Served Us Nachos, uses the first letter of each word as a memory cue. In the past, we included the dwarf planet of Pluto (so it was My Very Excellent Mother Just Served Us Nine Pizzas).

Create a Memory Palace

Another way that people memorize large amounts of information effectively is using a technique called a "memory palace" or the method of loci. I talk about this technique in Chapter 3 when I discuss analogies between memory and technology. In this technique, you use a very familiar path in a very familiar location as a structure to organize your memorization – for example, the rooms of your house. You do not have to think deeply about this space to remember. Then, mentally navigate through each room. This technique can also support memorizing things in order, because you can start from the front of the house and work your way to the back. Thus, if you are trying to remember a grocery list, you can start by mentally putting the bananas by the front door, and then the loaf of bread in the mud room or foyer, and then the peanut butter in the living room, etc.

This is a well-known and ancient technique going back to the ancient Greeks. Using imagery when placing your items in their locations makes this technique more effective, as I discuss in the strategy for using auditory and visual imagery to make things more memorable. The more unusual or bizarre the visual image, the more likely you are to remember it later.

If You Have Lost Something, Retrace Your Steps

In the earlier chapters of this book I talk about analogies to explain memory. Many people use spatial references to talk about memory, such as storing things in a particular spot. These references improve our understanding of memory and give us cues to boost retrieval. If you have lost your keys, for example, it is very helpful to retrace your steps. The reason that this works is due to the reconstructive nature of memory. Seeing the cues from the prior locations helps you to bring back the intention that you created in the first place. This common experience of forgetting something, retracing steps and then finding it is also related to why we sometimes walk into a room and forget why we went there.

Memories can be created through goals, intentions, and attention. If you are busy doing something and are thinking about multiple things at the same time, it can be easy to switch your attention from thought to thought. You may start with a goal, such as "look for my keys in the kitchen" but then be distracted by another thought or another goal, such as "pick up the pile of mail in the hallway and sort through it". In a familiar environment, such as your own home, you do not need to use high-level focused attention to go from one place to another. You can accomplish this task on auto pilot. This continuum of automatic to controlled processing that I discuss in Chapter 5, the chapter on attention, explains how we can walk into a room and not remember why. We formed an intention, got distracted, and then went on auto pilot while navigating through the house. Thus, retracing steps is very effective at bringing the retrieval cues into focus and reminding you of what you were thinking before you walked into that room. It also helps to reinstate the earlier context to help you to find your missing item.

Use Retrieval Practice

One of the ways that college students are using AI tools is to help them with different types of studying. Certain tasks, such as memorizing the steps of the Krebs cycle for an advanced biology course, contain details that simply have to be memorized verbatim. This type of material is different from the style of studying for an early European History course, where you may have to write an essay comparing different times in history. Students use AI tools to enhance their understanding at different levels (such as "explain this to me as though I were ten years old") and to generate mnemonics (tricks to boost memory, such as making up a song or using acronyms). While this can be helpful, there is another effect called the "generation effect"[15] and research has shown that students will be more likely to remember an acronym if they make it up themselves. However, the beneficial effects of generating study materials may not be the same in younger children[16].

Relationships between the Generation Effect and Retrieval Practice

Retrieval practice is a technique that has been studied extensively in college student populations, with a bit less research on younger students[17]. One of the key differences in retrieval practice, compared to other techniques to enhance learning, is that the focus is not on the "front end" or the encoding of the material. Rather, the focus is on the act of trying to remember information that has recently been learned. The act of trying to pull something from your memory is critical to the learning process. This view of focusing on retrieval is a relatively new way to think about learning and it goes beyond improving encoding. It is a very effective and active technique.

When they take a test in the classroom, children need to retrieve information from their memory. If they have repeatedly tried to do this through retrieval practice, they will have strengthened the pathways in the brain and should be able to access the information that they need effectively. One way I describe this to college students is, "In the test next week, you will be asked questions about the chapters that we have covered. If you study by re-reading the chapter multiple times, you will have a good sense of where things are in the book, and how they look on the page.

However, this practice of re-reading is not as helpful as you might think. If I were to give you the book during the exam and ask you to tell me where to find the keywords on the page, you would do very well. But instead, I'm going to ask you to define the keywords and apply them to different scenarios. Thus, re-reading does not match the format of the test and so it is less likely to help you. What will help you is to practice retrieving the keywords. Can you define them without looking at the book or your notes? If the answer is no, then that is what you should be practicing. Make flashcards and review them repeatedly (don't look at the answers, but guess if you do not know). Or read the text actively, such as reading a few pages, then closing the book and asking yourself what you just read. Could you describe the pages you just read to someone else?"

One recent study compared the active process of making predictions, which is related to the generation effect discussed above, and the active process of retrieval practice[18]. This comparison is important because we know that active learning is more engaging and can lead to better encoding and retention than passive forms of learning. The interaction of memory and attention discussed throughout this book is important here too. If children do not encode the information in the first place because their attention is directed elsewhere, it is very difficult for them to form new memories and learn new material.

The researchers compared two active techniques. Elementary school children from six to nine years of age were taught science lessons about insects, and then divided into two groups. One group made predictions about which of two items shown on a computer screen were insects before being told critical defining features of insects, such as having six legs or being hard on the outside. The children in the retrieval practice group were shown the defining information first and then were asked to select the picture on the screen that corresponded to the insect.

In the immediate learning phase, the children in the generating predictions group made more errors than in the retrieval practice group, which is not very surprising. Retrieval practice was more effective in the post-test that followed the learning phase as well. This finding about the benefits of retrieval practice has been replicated across studies on elementary school children, older children and college students.

As is often the case, there were some important nuances to be considered. This type of research is very important for helping us to develop learning strategies for children with different learning profiles. The generating predictions manipulation helped to increase encoding through more attentional focus on the materials, and this was determined by measuring the looking times of the children. When children had more attentional focus on the materials, performance in the generating predictions group did not differ from retrieval practice. These findings suggest that younger children benefit more from retrieval practice than from generating predictions, but that older children such as the nine-year-olds in this study may be equally likely to benefit from retrieval practice and from generating predictions. These findings offer helpful strategies to give teachers more tools and ways to mix up learning formats when introducing new material to students.

Use Cues and Reminders to Support Memory

Immediate memory has limits yet at the same time, long-term memory is almost limitless (see Chapter 8, myth #5). Technology can help with offloading, but it cannot take the place of learning.

Adults can help children to prepare themselves for each day, so that they can minimize forgetting. It is also important for children to learn that being distracted while doing a task or trying to remember something can cause forgetting. Children can be taught to use external systems, or what we call **cognitive offloading**, to build in reminders. Cognitive offloading is a method of using external prompts like sticky notes or technology as reminders. It "offloads" the cognitive responsibility to maintain the reminder over time because it is now located externally. Many families use a system of having one place in the home for school bags or other school supplies, so that the child must walk past the items needed for school before they leave home. Others encourage their children to review their school assignments in their planner or online software system the night before to ensure nothing is forgotten. As children get older, they become better at using cues and reminders and learn that if they structure their environment to support their memory, they are less likely to forget things. Research on metacognition and the use of cognitive offloading[19] indicates that by six or seven years of age, children begin to use reminders and other strategies much more than younger children. While metacognitive abilities emerge around three years of age, translating that awareness into strategies to minimize forgetting is not very effective in four- and five-year-old children. However, with each year of additional development, children improve in their awareness and understanding of both their metacognitive abilities and their effectiveness of using cognitive offloading to support their memory and attention. This improvement ultimately helps with forgetting as well.

Set Aside Focused Time for Learning and Allow for Breaks

Learning requires time and energy. It is important to allow students time to absorb new material, reflect on it, and make connections to things they already know. Attention and memory work closely together and if you are having trouble focusing on the material, it impairs your ability to make strong memories. Short breaks can facilitate a reset of your attentional focus. Children differ in their motivation on a given day or based on a given topic, and this is not necessarily a bad thing. It does not imply that children's attentional abilities are weaker overall than those of adults. A child can have an "off day" just as an adult can. It is important to recognize that children may need to set a time limit to enhance focus (say 30 minutes for older children and teenagers) and then take a ten-minute break. Each child will have an amount of time that works best for them, with some maintaining focus for up to an hour at a time.

This idea of working for a certain amount of focused time and then taking a break can also be applied in the classroom. Teachers working with younger children may find that 15 minutes of intense focus may be the maximum that can be sustained without a break. At present there is not an exact way to measure someone's maximum sustained attention limit, but it has been demonstrated that children can sustain their attentional focus for long periods under certain conditions. It is also important to consider a child's emotions and motivation on a given day.

This interconnected relationship between memory and attention is important[20]. Deep learning cannot happen efficiently if the learner is switching back and forth between different apps or distractions. This "switching cost" is why students should set a time limit for focused work, but also take breaks. A child who completes 30 minutes of focused work with no disruptions is in a better position than one who spends an hour working with interruptions. In terms of creating good connections with the material and generating good cues to support later recall, focused efforts are more fruitful, even if shorter in duration.

The Role of Nature in Resetting Attention

The role of nature in taking a break has much anecdotal support. Think of how younger children benefit from "recess". One of my children's teachers used to allocate ten minutes after recess for the children to put their heads down on their desks, or just rest quietly, before resuming their learning. These practices show children that learning requires cognitive effort and sustained focus, and that breaks can be restorative.

One way this has been studied experimentally is through Attention Restoration Theory (ART)[21], which discusses the ways in which being in nature, viewing nature scenes, or even having plants in the room can help restore mental energy. The theory was originally proposed in relation to adults and the differences between the stress levels of urban environments and more natural environments; however, it has been expanded to include studies on schoolchildren.

As discussed, focused attention is a cognitive process that requires effort and cannot be sustained indefinitely. Taking a break to relax and refresh the cognitive system is important for maintaining the ability to learn and take in new information. ART theory discusses the idea that going into nature or viewing nature scenes encourages a "soft fascination" as opposed to a type of intense concentration that requires more cognitive effort. This shift to a different type of processing can allow a sort of reset or refreshing, enabling a person to continue to perform cognitive tasks. Research that examines this view in children is being conducted, but it is still in the early stages. The conclusions thus far suggest that ART is applicable to children and that nature breaks are effective for children too[22].

A review of 12 recent studies found that children benefited from different types of nature-related activities, and that working memory and attention functioning showed improvement, relative to control groups in a built environment like a school courtyard. The studies included different measurements of working memory, such as the backwards digit span task, and different aspects of attentional functions, such as sustained attention and avoiding distractions from irrelevant features of a task.

While the outcome of this review is very promising, more work needs to be done. We need to understand what mechanisms might support the improvements in cognition so that we can explore the brain areas where these effects occur. We also need to understand if these positive findings about nature exposure apply broadly to all students or if there are certain populations that might benefit more than others, and how children of different ages may respond differently to nature-based activities. Nonetheless, the idea that exposure to and/or activities in nature can assist with attention and working memory functions is an easy-to-implement and low-cost way to help people reset and get the most out of their cognitive systems.

Study In a Quiet Place or with Instrumental Background Music

As part of the recommendation to set up your environment to maximize learning, it is important to recognize the role of the sounds around you. Listening to music with lyrics can be disruptive to reading comprehension. Find a way to study that optimizes your concentration and minimizes distractions.

Take individual and developmental differences into account. Younger children have more difficulty with attention control and maintain focused attention for less time than older children. They also have a smaller memory capacity.

Part of being a self-regulated learner is knowing if your study environment is helping or hindering your progress. Some students need the additional boost of motivation from seeing people around them studying. They thrive in a coffee shop environment because it gives them additional stimulation and motivation. Other students need complete silence and isolation to be able to focus. Take note that research has repeatedly shown that music with lyrics is harmful to many tasks, including reading and studying[23].

Structure Learning Activities in the Classroom with Age-Appropriate Support

A long time ago, many adults thought that children were just like them, but smaller. This point of view does not recognize that there are many more changes going on in child development than physical growth alone. Cognition develops, along with emotions and social skills, to support a broad array of changes in childhood. Thus, children are more than just "small versions of adults".

We know that working memory is an important factor in learning and in academic achievement. Working memory capacity is limited to about four items in adults[24], and is lower in young children. This information should be used to structure materials and learning in the classroom. Just as early word skills and vocabulary development are important for reading, early numeracy skills have been investigated to gain a better understanding how children's quantitative skills can be improved. One promising area of research is the use of gestures to support early math learning and assist with the development of numeracy skills[25] in young children. Gestures can be as simple as counting on fingers or can include directions, such as pointing upwards to indicate that a number is increasing. There are also brief interventions that include parent-child training[26] on the use of gestures to support math learning in children as young as three to five.

As discussed in other sections of this book, longitudinal research is one of the ways that researchers learn about techniques that can improve a specific skill or ability. To investigate numeracy skills, researchers worked with kindergarten children in the US ranging in age from five to seven years. The children were divided into four groups and randomly assigned in classrooms to the different groups. This random assignment in classrooms helped to control for any outcomes related to the effect of the individual teacher, which we know from previous research on metacognitive language in the classroom can have an impact on student outcomes. The children were given pretests to assess their baseline mathematical and numeracy skills. Then, a two-week intervention took place across the four groups. The control group participated in activities that supported reading, such as playing word games, and did not do anything math or number related. The other three groups used either finger-based games to learn about math concepts, manipulation-based games such as using tokens or chips to assist them, or a combination of finger and manipulation-based games. Overall, all three experimental groups showed greater improvement from the pre-test to the post-test than the control group. This suggests that all the techniques support learning at the global level.

However, when the children were further divided into lower and higher-performing groups based upon the math pre-test, the outcomes were more nuanced. The gains from the finger-based games were larger for the children with lower performance at the start. The gains from the manipulation-based games and the combined games were greater for those with higher performance at the start. The lower- and higher-performing children also differed on a measure of spatial working memory, again suggesting the importance of working memory in supporting academic behaviors. The conclusions suggest that active games that include fingers and manipulation can benefit students overall, but that it is also important to consider the individual characteristics of the students. This point comes up repeatedly throughout the literature reviewed in this book.

Consider the Benefits of Spaced Retrieval

Another important element of learning is a concept known as spaced retrieval. Learning information all at one time is not as effective for long-term learning as spacing it out over multiple study sessions. Spacing out the learning sessions helps to create more enduring memory traces and allows for the creation of more memory cues. Teachers are putting spaced retrieval into action very successfully in the classroom.

One notable example was in a middle-school English class. How do you teach middle schoolers new vocabulary words? How can a teacher help them to move from the bottom of Bloom's taxonomy, simple memorization, to the higher levels of learning that involve comprehension and application of knowledge? The method I observed included repeating material across the week in different formats. At the beginning of a new unit, the teacher introduced the words on vocabulary worksheets. They started out with the definitions. Then, as the unit went on, the class continued to work on the same words but included different activities and ways to interact with the words. The children had to use the words in sentences, match them to similar words, compare the word meanings, and complete a series of worksheets across the unit with different assignments due on different days. The unit, typically lasting about one week, concluded with a quiz on the words. This distributed (or spaced) retrieval, coupled with different levels of encoding and engaging with the words, helps the students to move up the levels of Bloom's taxonomy while also giving retrieval practice. This scaffolded and structured learning works well for middle-school students. Older students can apply their more advanced knowledge structures and metacognition to tasks like these as well and may not need as much scaffolding (depending on the difficulty level of the content).

An example from a high-school science class provides some scaffolding but not as much as middle-school students might need. Structured outlines can be provided by the teacher in class. The students can complete them together with the teacher to provide the first exposure to new content and become familiar with the materials. Then, using the textbook and structured outlines, the students are asked to complete another outline, but this time it is provided by the textbook. This process provides opportunities to space out the learning, and helps the students identify the important concepts and make connections between them. In addition, this process allows repetition by having the students complete the activities for teacher-based content and then with textbook-based content. These activities include ways to direct attention to the material with the appropriate level of scaffolding. The students must complete the outlines in real time yet are given guidance so that they are not left on their own to determine what content to emphasize. The process also helps them to build their knowledge base by making connections to the content and enhances their understanding of the material by hearing about it and seeing it from the related but different points of view of the teacher and the textbook.

These two examples are effective because they provide age-appropriate support and methods to direct the students' attention. There are several other ways that K-12 teachers effectively combine their content knowledge and their skills to produce successful learning environments. Author Jose Bowen[27] makes an excellent analogy between the role of the teacher and the role of a physical trainer. A person can join a gym and hire a personal trainer, but the personal trainer cannot do the exercises for them. In the same way, a teacher can provide the content and structure for learning new information but cannot learn the information for the student. Learning, like building physical fitness, takes time and energy. Teachers act as "cognitive coaches" and give students the opportunity to learn. However, it is ultimately up to the student to do the work.

Take-Home Points

- You can learn in multiple modalities; why limit yourself to just one?
- Believe that you can learn.
- Take the time to make things memorable by making connections to other ideas or related concepts. Younger children are building

their vocabularies and they do not have access to as many words as adults do.
- Connect the content to something personal and use emotion to your advantage.
- Get good sleep.
- Use visual and/or auditory imagery when learning something new.
- When you need to memorize, break up information into groups of items and/or make acronyms.
- If you have lost something, retrace your steps.
- Use retrieval practice. The act of retrieval strengthens the pathways in the brain and facilitates future recall. Retrieval is not a passive process.
- Use cues and reminders to support memory.
- Set aside focused time for learning and allow for breaks.
- Study in a quiet place or with instrumental background music.
- Structure learning activities in the classroom with age-appropriate supports that take into account how memory and attention change with age.
- Consider the benefits of spaced retrieval.

Chapter Summary

Strategies such as involving multiple senses when learning, as opposed to focusing more narrowly on one sense, can be very effective in creating more retrieval cues for new material. Take the time to make things memorable by making connections to other ideas or related concepts, or to something personally relevant or interesting. Sleep matters not only for the physical benefits, but because it allows time for the brain to consolidate memories. Retrieval practice is a powerful tool for boosting memory performance. These are some concrete methods for recognizing the processes of memory and attention and how to apply them in real life.

Notes

1 Keppel, G., & Underwood, B. J. (1962). Proactive inhibition in short-term retention of single items. *Journal of Verbal Learning & Verbal Behavior, 1*(3), 153–161. https://doi.org/10.1016/S0022-5371(62)80023-1
2 Dzulkifli, M. A., & Halim, A. Z. A. (2023). Input modality and its effect on memory recall. *Journal of Cognitive Sciences and Human Development*, (2). https://doi.org/10.33736/jcshd.5699.2023
3 McGuire, S. Y. (2023). *Teach yourself how to learn: Strategies you can use to ace any course at any level*. Taylor & Francis.

4 Collins, A. M. & Loftus, E. F. (1975). A spreading-activation theory of semantic processing. *Psychological Review, 82*(6), 407–428. https://doi.org/10.1037/0033-295X.82.6.407
5 Cox, C. R. & Haebig, E. (2023). Child-oriented word associations improve models of early word learning. *Behavior Research Methods, 55*, 16–37. https://doi.org/10.3758/s13428-022-01790-y
6 Rizzuto, T. E., Cherry, K. E. & LeDoux, J. A. (2012). The aging process and cognitive capabilities, in W. C. Borman & J. W. Hedge (Eds), *The Oxford Handbook of work and aging*. Oxford Library of Psychology. https://doi.org/10.1093/oxfordhb/9780195385052.013.0092
7 Lang, J. M. (2020). *Distracted: Why students can't focus and what you can do about it.* Basic Books.
8 Whitehouse, A. J., Maybery, M. T. & Durkin, K. (2006). The development of the picture-superiority effect. *British Journal of Developmental Psychology, 24*(4), 767–773. https://doi.org/10.1348/026151005X74153
9 Paivio, A. (1991). Dual coding theory: Retrospect and current status. *Canadian Journal of Psychology, 45*, 255–287. https://doi.org/10.1037/h0084295
10 Slotnick, S. D., Thompson, W. L. & Kosslyn, S. M. (2012). Visual memory and visual mental imagery recruit common control and sensory regions of the brain. *Cognitive Neuroscience, 3*(1), 14–20. https://doi.org/10.1080/17588928.2011.578210
11 Hahn, M., Joechner, A. K., Roell, J., Schabus, M., Heib, D. P., Gruber, G., ... & Hoedlmoser, K. (2019). Developmental changes of sleep spindles and their impact on sleep-dependent memory consolidation and general cognitive abilities: A longitudinal approach. *Developmental Science, 22*(1), e12706. https://doi.org/10.1111/desc.12706
12 Do, A. H., Schnitker, S. A. & Scullin, M. K. (2025). Gratitude, flourishing and prosocial behaviors following experimental sleep restriction and sleep extension. *The Journal of Positive Psychology, 20*(4), 604–615. https://doi.org/10.1080/17439760.2024.2394452
13 Paruthi, S., Brooks, L. J., D'Ambrosio, C., Hall, W. A., Kotagal, S., Lloyd, R. M., Malow, B. A., Maski, K., Nichols, C., Quan, S. F., Rosen, C. L., Troester, M. M. & Wise, M. S. (2016). Recommended amount of sleep for pediatric populations: A consensus statement of the American Academy of Sleep Medicine. *Journal of Clinical Sleep Medicine, 12*(6), 785–786. http://dx.doi.org/10.5664/jcsm.5866
14 Reynolds, A. M., Spaeth, A. M., Hale, L., Williamson, A. A., LeBourgeois, M. K., Wong, S. D., ... & Carskadon, M. A. (2023). Pediatric sleep: current knowledge, gaps, and opportunities for the future. *Sleep, 46*(7). https://doi.org/10.1093/sleep/zsad060.
15 Graf, P. (1982). The memorial consequences of generation and transformation. *Journal of Verbal Learning & Verbal Behavior, 21*(5), 539–548. https://doi.org/10.1016/S0022-5371(82)90764-2
16 Brod, G. (2021). Generative learning: Which strategies for what age? *Educational Psychology Review, 33*, 1295–1318 (2021). https://doi.org/10.1007/s10648-020-09571-9
17 Fazio, L. K., & Marsh, E. J. (2019). Retrieval-based learning in children. *Current Directions in Psychological Science, 28*(2), 111–116. https://doi.org/10.1177/0963721418806673
18 Carvalho, P. F. & Godwin, K. E. (2024). Comparing generating predictions with retrieval practice as learning strategies for primary school children. *Journal of Experimental Psychology: Applied, 31*(2), 71–83. https://doi.org/10.1037/xap0000523

19 Armitage, K. L., Gilbert, S. J. (2025). The nature and development of cognitive offloading in children. *Child Development Perspectives, 19(2),* 108–115. https://doi.org/10.1111/cdep.12532

20 Cowan, N., Bao, C., Bishop-Chrzanowski, B. M., Costa, A. N., Greene, N. R., Guitard, D., ... & Ünal, Z. E. (2024). The relation between attention and memory. *Annual Review of Psychology, 75*(1), 183–214. https://doi.org/10.1146/annurev-psych-040723-012736

21 Kaplan S. (1995). The restorative benefits of nature: Toward an integrative framework. *Journal of Environmental Psychology, 15,* 169–182. https://doi.org/10.1016/0272-4944(95)90001-2

22 Vella-Brodrick, D. A. & Gilowska, K. (2022). Effects of nature (greenspace) on cognitive functioning in school children and adolescents: A systematic review. *Educational Psychology Review, 34*(3), 1217–1254. https://doi.org/10.1007/s10648-022-09658-5

23 Christopher, E. A. & Shelton, J. T. (2017). Individual differences in working memory predict the effect of music on student performance. *Journal of Applied Research in Memory and Cognition,* 6(2), 167–173. https://doi.org/10.1016/j.jarmac.2017.01.012

24 Cowan, N. (2010). The magical mystery four: How is working memory capacity limited, and why? *Current Directions in Psychological Science, 19*(1), 51–57. https://doi.org/10.1177/0963721409359277

25 Kovarsky, R. G., & Congdon, E. L. (2026). A handy tool: Using fingers as a numerical representation specifically benefits lower performers in kindergarten mathematics. *Developmental Psychology, 62*(4), 802–816. https://doi.org/10.1037/dev0002032

26 Barkin, R., Grose, G. E., Krishnasamy, N., Scalise, N. R. & Ramani, G. B. (2025). Helping hands: Encouraging parent-child gestures during informal mathematics activities. *Journal of Applied Developmental Psychology, 99,* 101827. https://doi.org/10.1016/j.appdev.2025.101827

27 Bowen, J. A. (2021). *Teaching change: How to develop independent thinkers using relationships, resilience, and reflection*. JHU Press.

Chapter 10

Final Conclusions and Take-Home Messages

The goal of this book is to increase parents', teachers', and professionals' awareness of memory and attention functions in children and to provide helpful, scientifically based strategies to improve learning outcomes. As you learned how the brain functions, how memory and attention are closely interconnected, and how forgetting can be experienced in different ways, I hope that you came to understand yourself and the children around you in a new light. I also hope that discussing some of the myths of memory has made it easier to understand the truth about memory functions. Small shifts in the way that we use reminders and design our learning environments can lead to big outcomes. Knowing how to increase our attentional focus and retain information better can give us a better idea of how to manage our precious cognitive resources and engage our efforts in the most effective way.

Memory is a critical piece of being human. We rely on it every minute of every day, as it helps us to understand ourselves. We are often annoyed when we do not remember something, yet we fail to celebrate the many memory successes that occur regularly. In the same way, I believe that we often underestimate and underappreciate the multiple feats of memory and attention that children accomplish daily. Considering the complex functioning of the memory system along with the fact that we build knowledge upon existing facts and neural network connections, it is incredible to realize the many ways that children acquire competencies. The importance of children's ability to create new knowledge and to build a foundation of skills and abilities that will serve them in the future cannot be overstated. Everything that they experience starts out as something new, and it takes longer to build new knowledge from the ground up. It is no wonder that younger children need the most sleep.

Learning early on about the strong interconnections between their memory and attention systems helps children succeed in any path they choose. Knowing how researchers have studied memory and attentional processes can shed light on daily tasks. I discussed the basics of brain functioning and how experimental research and case studies have taught us about the structures of

DOI: 10.4324/9781003672814-13

memory and attention. I also discussed some historical references to memory, and how analogies about memory have changed over time.

Technology has played a large role in the way that people talk about memory processes, and that trend continues today. AI systems emerged around the same time as the field of cognitive psychology in the 1950s, and the two fields of study continue to inform each other as new developments arise. I discussed different types of memory, although not all, and how understanding which parts of your memory system are involved in different tasks can increase how well you remember information in the future. As another example, knowing that to retain new information you must pay attention to it in the first place may sound basic, but it is critical.

Knowing that memory is an interconnected system that involves multiple aspects of brain function helps us to maximize our experiences and actively engage with learning. This knowledge also helps us to appreciate the different ways that forgetting can occur. Using retrieval practice to identify the knowledge you have is also important for identifying areas that may need additional review. The close relationships between our memory and cognitive systems can give us insight into what we may be more likely to remember, and also more likely to forget.

Many teachers already know how to connect with students in the classroom without being taught about memory and attention. Yet it could make their jobs a bit easier if children were given the opportunity to understand themselves better at an earlier age. I have great respect for teachers and want to support their mission, as they have incredibly important roles in our children's lives. As technology continues to evolve at a rapid pace, the ability to learn how to learn is at a premium. Children are excellent at learning new things and picking up new skills. As just one example of this versatility, think about how young children can acquire a first and a second language. The amount of effort that a five-year-old child must exert to learn a second language is much less that of an adult. Anyone who has tried to learn a second language in their 20s, 30s, or 40s can attest to this experience. Yet young children pick up languages with ease. They are likely to adapt to technology in ways that we have not imagined. I look forward to seeing what exciting new pathways will emerge as children are given the tools to interface with technology in new ways.

Having said that, I believe we must be aware of the guardrails that children may need to facilitate their learning. Many schools in the K-12 space have implemented complete phone bans and have limited the ways in which children can access information on browsers or other information systems. I accept these policies because I understand that teachers, principals, and educational leaders must regularly deal with many challenges. The point I want to emphasize is that the daily lives of children outside the school environment will involve technology, and it may or may not have any guardrails.

I see this when new first-year students report to college after experiencing technology bans in their high schools. The level of freedom and autonomy is sometimes overwhelming, as some students have not developed effective strategies for dealing with the distractions from their phones or other social media. Knowing that they can bring their tablet, their laptop, and their phone to class and no one will stop them can be invigorating; however, having multiple potential sources of distraction is not the best way to retain the information being presented in the classroom. Helping children to develop metacognitive skills and become self-regulated learners will help them navigate the changing landscape of these new technologies.

Knowing that memory does not work like a recording device can help people to develop strategies to engage their memory and attention and to use devices (such as textbooks, notes, and videos of relevant content) to revisit the information. Being aware that individuals differ in how long they can sustain their attentional focus, and that this is not necessarily a bad thing, is important.

Children's ability to sustain attention and switch between different tasks or assignments develops over time. The younger the child, the more external supports they need to navigate these tasks. Older children need to be reminded that working hard on an assignment or a reading can take time and energy. I highly recommend that children determine how they work best and set up an environment for studying or learning that works for them and minimizes distractions. Then, when it is time for a break, going into a different space, like a walk around the neighborhood or a quick trip to the kitchen for a snack, breaks up their study time and helps their attention processes to recover from the effort.

Many professionals are working diligently to spread knowledge about memory to as many people as possible. As society continues to gain more access to information, it will not necessarily become easier for children to learn. In fact, we may need to provide more guidance on how to evaluate sources and separate the credible ones from the alternative, as just one aspect of the information highway that we travel. Fortunately, there are many excellent books and podcasts by experts who have worked in the intersection of cognitive psychology and learning. The people who have most influenced me in my own journey of teaching and learning in higher education have come from different disciplines, like Chemistry, English and Music; in part, this is because these authors and educators do such a good job of explaining complex cognitive psychology constructs in language that everyone can understand.

Thinking about the overall direction of technology and children's development brings many questions to the minds of parents, teachers, and caregivers, for example on childhood cognitive development. We have so much more to learn about the human brain and the way that children develop their cognitive and metacognitive abilities. We still cannot build an exact model of the human brain, place it in a robot, and have that robot demonstrate human-level understanding, empathy, and adaptation to changes in the environment. The human brain is much more complex and multifaceted than any machine that exists today. While enormous leaps in technology are happening around us, there is still much that we do not know. It is an exciting time to support children and to help them learn about memory, attention, and learning.

Take-Home Points

- Children are very successful with daily memory and attention. As adults, we tend to focus on memory failures. Instead, we should acknowledge our numerous memory successes.
- Memory and attention are interconnected systems. Younger children need more time to encode information than older children and adults and are actively building their networks of knowledge. It is not surprising that they need more sleep.
- Many resources combine effective teaching practices with knowledge of how human memory and attention systems function.
- Technology is changing rapidly, yet there is still much that is not known about the human memory system. Children adapt very easily and will teach us how to interact with new technologies in different ways.

Chapter Summary

In this chapter I discussed the final conclusions and take-home messages of this book. I reviewed some topics, including the basics of brain structure and function, analogies to explain memory, and the differences among several types of memory. I also reviewed the importance of attention for successful encoding and the fact that there are different types of forgetting. People develop their metacognition and memory skills in childhood and can apply this knowledge to learn more effectively. They also interact with AI systems and will create new knowledge through these interactions. Knowing the differences between myths and truths about memory and attention can help children and adults to reach their cognitive potential.

Glossary of Terms

Chapter 2

Amygdala: a brain structure located in the middle of the brain, below the cortex, that helps us to process emotions

Anterograde amnesia: a type of memory loss that reaches forward in time. Individuals with anterograde amnesia are unable to form new memories but may retain memories from their past.

Attention: although this term is difficult to define precisely, one way to think of it is as the current contents of a person's consciousness. What is someone aware of right now, in the current moment? Attention helps children and adults concentrate their efforts and allocate cognitive resources towards a goal.

Contralateral functioning: the two hemispheres of the brain are organized by this principle of controlling the opposite side of the body. The right hemisphere of the brain controls movement on the left side of the body, for example.

Cortex: the outermost layer of the brain. It comes from a word meaning "bark", as in tree bark.

Encoding: the process of taking in details in your environment with the intention of remembering them later. It is closely linked with attention.

Glia cells: cells in the brain that support the neurons and assist with neuronal communication

Gray matter: part of the outermost layer of the brain. It is made up mostly of cell bodies and axons that are not myelinated

Hippocampus: a brain structure located in the middle of the brain, below the cortex, that is critically important for the process of transferring memories from the short term to the long term

Lateralization of function: the organization of brain into two hemispheres. Each side of the brain is involved with certain processes. The left hemisphere of the brain, for example, controls the right side of the body.

Myelin sheath: a part of the neuron. It is the covering of the axon that insulates signals as they travel down the axon. It is also referred to as white matter.

Neuron: the basic unit of the nervous system or the nerve cells of the brain

Neurotransmitters: chemical signals that allow for signals to be sent from one neuron to another

Plasticity: the ability of the brain to change in response to experience with the environment. Learning occurs through plasticity.

Retrieval: the active process of rebuilding a memory from different memory traces stored in different locations in the brain

Retrograde amnesia: a type of memory loss that affects memories from the past

Synapses: gaps between neurons that facilitate neuronal communication

Thalamus: a sub-cortical brain structure that acts as a relay station for most sensory signals

Chapter 3

Artificial intelligence: a computer system that mimics aspects of human intelligence by using networks of information

Cognitive Psychology: a branch of psychology that focuses on thinking, decision-making, reasoning, language, memory, and attention. Cognitive psychologists study how people think, and how certain processes work in the brain.

Large language models (LLM): a type of artificial intelligence system that was originally based upon language and can be trained with large data sets to make predictions

Memory palace: a method of memorizing, also called "method of loci". People use a familiar place, such as their home or their neighborhood, and place images of items to be remembered along a well-known mental path.

Meta-analysis: an analysis of multiple published research papers using clearly established, objective procedures to produce summary statements about the results of many papers, as opposed to the results of any one single peer-reviewed paper

Chapter 4

Declarative memory: a subset of long-term memory. It also called verbalizable memory or explicit memory. It is subdivided into episodic and semantic long-term memory.

Episodic memory: the type of long-term memory that is unique to each individual person and is based on their own life experiences, such as a memory of their birthday party

False memory: the tendency for children and adults participating in a memory experiment to report that they have previously seen a word in a word list that was not there. We learn and maintain semantic information in networks, such as the idea that a canary is a bird.

Highly superior autobiographical memory: also known as hyperthymesia. The unique ability of some people to remember precise details of individual moments in their lives.

Long-term memory: the vast storehouse of information from a person's life. It has a long duration and a potentially unlimited capacity, in the sense that it is unlikely that a person's brain could ever get full.

Procedural memory: a type of long-term memory that is non-declarative or non-verbalizable. It is often thought of in terms of highly practiced skills and habits and is sometimes called muscle memory.

Saccades: rapid eye movements that help to bring items into the central focus of visual attention

Semantic memory: the type of long-term memory that is based upon facts and information and is shared with others, such as the name of the first President of the US.

Sensory memory: a type of memory that is based upon taking information in through the senses. It has a large capacity for storage but a very brief duration.

Short-term memory: a type of memory that is based upon a person's current experience and lasts about 30 seconds. It has a capacity limit of about seven plus or minus two items when the person can refresh or rehearse the material to keep it active.

Working memory: a more active version of short-term memory. It is based on a person's current experiences and plans and is updated in real time in response to task demands. The capacity limit of working memory is about four plus or minus one item.

Chapter 5

Divided attention: a situation in which a person moves their attentional focus rapidly between more than one task, or type of information, such as trying to listen to someone speaking while doing something else at the same time.

Multitasking: doing two tasks at the same time, such as cooking while listening to music. Depending on the two tasks, it may be possible to do both at the same time but very often there is rapid shifting of attention between the two tasks.

Sustained attention: when a child or adult maintains their current attentional focus on one task or event without interruption

Chapter 6

Episodic future thinking: using mental imagery or other methods to think about a future task, such as imagining stopping on the way home from work to pick up milk.

Metacognition: often described as thinking about thinking. It can involve both the control of cognition, such as using a strategy, and the monitoring of cognition, such as realizing a person needs to slow down to do a task correctly.

Metamemory: knowledge about a person's own memory abilities

Proactive interference: a type of forgetting based on the similarity of information reaching forward in time and making something more difficult to remember

Prospective memory: a type of memory that involves planning to do something in the future

Retroactive interference: a type of forgetting based on the similarity of information reaching back in time and making something more difficult to remember

Retrospective memory: a type of memory that involves retrieving an event or experience from the past

Chapter 7

Executive functioning: a broad term that encompasses multiple types of complex behaviors like inhibiting responses, working memory, and shifting from one task to another

Open Science methods: actions of researchers to increase transparency and to share research practices, data, and analyses with the public and with other researchers

Self-regulated learning: a subcomponent of metacognition that involves behaviors like analyzing a task and setting goals to accomplish that task and then going back to evaluate if the goals are being met

Sycophantic: the tone that some Gen AI systems use to respond to humans by being overly positive and encouraging, even when they are reporting incorrect information

Chapter 8

Bit: smallest unit of information in a digital format. Computers contain bits, or a binary digit, which can either be a zero or a one.

Brain training: interventions or other types of cognitive activities designed to improve overall cognitive functioning, such as solving puzzles, playing word games, or doing other types of challenging mental tasks

Byte: the next size up from a bit of digital information, which is typically eight bits.

Ecological validity: the idea that research has meaningful real-world outcomes, as opposed to research that is conducted in the laboratory setting and may not generalize as well to life outside of the lab

Far transfer: a way to assess if a training program or intervention has produced improved performance on a different task. If someone practiced a working memory task over time and got better at other cognitive tasks such as an academic achievement test, this could be evidence of far transfer.

Gigabyte (GB): a storage term in computing representing 1024 megabytes

Kilobyte (KB): a storage term in computing representing 1024 bytes

Megabyte (MB): a storage term in computing representing 1024 kilobytes

Near transfer: a way to assess if a training program or intervention has produced improved performance on a similar task. An example is practicing crossword puzzles and as a result increasing vocabulary scores.

Petabyte (PB): a storage term in computing representing 1024 terabytes

Replication: a process in scientific research that involves repeating a research project to determine if the same results can be obtained in a different research lab and with a different group of participants

Terabyte (TB): a storage term in computing representing 1024 gigabytes

Chapter 9

Cognitive economy: the idea that our mental systems and thinking sometimes rely upon shortcuts in processing or rely on previously learned information to streamline and facilitate new processing

Cognitive offloading: a method of using external tools such as writing notes or using reminders in a phone to reduce the burden of mental work on a person and placing it on a device or tool.

Generation effect: people remember items they generate themselves better than when given all the information to generate an item. An example is generating the second half of a word pair, such as fork:____, as opposed to being given the word pair fork: knife.

Mnemonics: memory tricks or strategies to make learning or memorizing easier, such as using acronyms to learn a list of items

Retrieval practice: the act of retrieving information as a form of learning and studying, as opposed to a passive practice like re-reading notes.

Semantic network: an organizational principle of semantic memory. Information is organized in meaningfully related structures, such as keeping all information about birds together in memory. The features of birds (beaks, feathers etc.) are also part of the semantic network.

Sleep dependent memory consolidation: sleep helps a person to retain information and can make memories stronger by allowing time for processes in the hippocampus to happen. These effects have been measured by a tool called a polysomnogram that measures electrical activity in the brain when people are sleeping. In the second stage of non-REM sleep, an electrical profile called a sleep spindle has been linked to learning and memory during sleep.

Spaced retrieval: the practice of studying over periods of time, as opposed to massed practice such as cramming. Dividing up study time over several days is more likely to lead to long-term retention than cramming.

Recommended Resources for Interested Readers

Agarwal, P. K. (Ed.) (2025). *Smart teaching stronger learning*. Unleash Learning Press.
Agarwal, P. K., & Bain, P. M. (2024). *Powerful teaching: Unleash the science of learning*. Wiley.
Bowen, J. A. (2021). *Teaching change: How to develop independent thinkers using relationships, resilience, and reflection*. JHU Press.
Bowen, J. A., & Watson, C. E. (2025). *Teaching with AI: A practical guide to a new era of human learning*. JHU Press.
Lang, J. M. (2020). *Distracted: Why students can't focus and what you can do about it.* Basic Books.
Lang, J. M. (2021). *Small teaching: Everyday lessons from the science of learning (2nd edition)*. Wiley.
Margulis, E. H. (2026). *Transported: The everyday magic of musical daydreams.* Liveright.
Mark, G. (2023). *Attention span: A groundbreaking way to restore balance, happiness and productivity*. Harlequin.
McGuire, S. Y. (2023). *Teach yourself how to learn: Strategies you can use to ace any course at any level*. Taylor & Francis.
Miller, M. D. (2022). *Remembering and forgetting in the age of technology: Teaching, learning, and the science of memory in a wired world.* West Virginia University Press.
Miller, M. D. (2027). *The attention spectrum*. Norton.
Overson, C. E., Hakala, C. M., Kordonowy, L. L., & Benassi, V. A. (Eds). (2023). *In their own words: What scholars and teachers want you to know about why and how to apply the science of learning in your academic setting*. Society for the Teaching of Psychology. https://teachpsych.org/ebooks/itow
Rhodes, M. G., Cleary, A. M., & DeLosh, E. L. (2020). *A guide to effective studying and learning: Practical strategies from the science of learning*. Oxford University Press.
Sumeracki, M., & Kaminske, A. N. (2024). *The psychology of memory*. Routledge.
Yeager, D. (2024). *10 to 25: The science of motivating young people*. Avid Reader Press.

There are some great resources from a faculty member at the University of Washington, Neuroscience for Kids[1], for teachers and educators who work with children, and who want to better understand the structure and function of the brain.

1 https://faculty.washington.edu/chudler/index1.html

Index

Note: Page numbers in *italics* indicate figures on the corresponding pages.

For Product Safety Concerns and Information please contact our EU
representative GPSR@taylorandfrancis.com
Taylor & Francis Verlag GmbH, Kaufingerstraße 24, 80331 München, Germany

www.ingramcontent.com/pod-product-compliance
Lightning Source LLC
LaVergne TN
LVHW010259051126
851780LV00028B/319
9781041140610